THE

Comfort

DINER

COOKBOOK

THE Comfort DINER
COOKBOOK

A World of Classic Diner Delights, from Homestyle Dinners to
Satisfying Breakfasts and Fun Midnight Treats

Ira Freehof with Pia Catton

clarkson potter/publishers
new york

CLARKSON N. POTTER is a trademark and POTTER and colophon are registered trademarks
of Random House, Inc.

Library of Congress Cataloging-in-Publication Data

Freehof, Ira.
The Comfort Diner cookbook/Ira Freehof with Pia Catton.—1st ed.
Includes index.
1. Cookery, American.   2. Comfort Diner (Restaurant)   I. Catton, Pia.   II. Title.
TX715.F8628 2005   2004028750
641.5973—dc22
ISBN 1-4000-8108-4

Printed in the United States

Design by Jan Derevjanik

10 9 8 7 6 5 4 3 2 1

First Edition

I'd like to dedicate this book to the four generations of women in my life: my grandmothers, Sylvia and Shirley, for showing me firsthand how wonderful home cooking could be and what an important ingredient love is for any recipe. They sparked my love of food. My mother, Mickie, encouraged me to discover the joy of cooking for myself, while at the same time showing me what an integral part of the family a kitchen table can be. My daughters, Brinley and Cara, continue to reward me by sitting at *our* kitchen table and sharing not only many of the dishes in this book but also their love of food and family. My wife, Sandy, has been incredible! She's been the special ingredient that has bonded these women to my heart and without her help, support, and love, the Comfort Diner's doors would have never opened.

—Ira Freehof

acknowledgments

I'd like to thank the entire staff of the Comfort Diner, past and present, especially those who have been there since the beginning: Chivo, Roger, and Lynn.

I'd also like to thank the thousands of customers who've supported us with their appetites, wallets, and, most importantly, with their hearts.

In the fall of 1995, restaurant designer David Rosencrans took my crayon drawings and a tour of classic diners. He then succeeded in making a new design with a fresh look, while at the same time paying homage to the past. Thank you, David.

I can't thank Karen Schloss and Frank Diaz enough for their encouragement, support, and friendship over the years. If you've ever heard of the Comfort Diner before this book, it is undoubtedly due to their efforts.

To my business partner, Greg: You've helped add to the success of the Comfort Diner. As our business has grown, so has our friendship and I thank you for both.

To my coauthor, Pia Catton: Thank you! Without you, this book would be nothing but the rambling thoughts going through my mind and some recipes written on the back of placemats, notepaper, and index cards. Out of that, you made this. Wow!

—Ira Freehof

I am enormously grateful to Ira Freehof, Karen Schloss, and Frank Diaz for the opportunity to be involved with this book. Many thanks are due to my agent Stacy Glick and to my editor, the sharp-eyed Adina Steiman, whose help I deeply appreciate. Thank you also to production editor Meghan Wilson, designer Jan Derevjanik, and production manager Linnea Knollmueller for all their hard work.

Eugenio "Chivo" de Los Santos and the Comfort Diner staff graciously put up with me week after week. Muchas gracias.

My boundless appreciation goes to Charlotte Ibarra, a true friend whose encouragement and frequent dish washing gave me fortitude. I'd like to thank my brother, Grant, who was always happy to be there, happy to help the ball club. Thank you also to my friends, family, and *New York Sun* colleagues who tested (and tasted) recipes and provided feedback.

And an obnoxiously loud, air-guitar salute goes to the folks at radio station Q104.3. You guys rock.

—Pia Catton

contents

Acknowledgments
Introduction

introduction

The motto at the Comfort Diner is a simple one: "Time to eat good food!"

That's because whenever you walk through its doors—no matter what time it is or how hungry you are—it's time for something good to eat. And my take on "good food" is not at all complicated. At the Comfort Diner we serve no-nonsense American fare that harkens back to the golden age of the diner. Think grilled cheese, meatloaf, burgers, fries, and milkshakes.

But we don't stop there. While my two Manhattan diners pay homage to the past, they're not limited by it. On our menu you'll see newfangled (but not highfalutin) American classics—like chopped salads and breakfast burritos—that would never have appeared at any diner in the '40s.

That's okay with me (and with our guests, too—the chopped salad happens to be our best-selling salad). My goal when I opened the first Comfort Diner in 1996 was not simply to replicate the diner-experience egg cream for egg cream. That would make the place a museum. Instead, I sought to bring high quality back to diner food, to create a cheerful atmosphere with a menu that is both nostalgic and up to date.

Well, the approach worked. New Yorkers welcomed the concept with ravenous appetites. In a short time, the place was packed. Named "Best Diner in New York" by *Time Out New York* and *The Resident,* the Comfort Diner was an instant success. In 1998, I opened my second Comfort Diner, and soon afterward, *Gourmet* magazine gave us a rave review. Over the years we've been covered in print by the *New York Times, Bon Appétit, Chocolatier, New York* magazine, and *Woman's Day.*

But it's not the great publicity that makes it all worthwhile. It's the little joys of running a restaurant. At a place like the Comfort Diner, you get to witness people from all walks of life enjoying the same culinary experience. Diners appeal to an amazing variety of people, so on any given day, we've got business people, families with small children, soon-to-be couples on first dates (I've noticed plenty taking place over the years), and maybe a celebrity or two (Harrison Ford, Jerry Seinfeld, George Clooney, Diane Sawyer, and Mike Nichols have all stopped by).

Another joy is seeing food trends come along—and then letting them go on their merry way. I don't know about you, but I think the world changes enough as it is. It's nice to know that some things stay the same: a BLT is always going to make me smile. I don't care if it's the year of the low-fat diet, the no-dairy plan, or the low-carb craze—when you need reassurance, a steamy chicken potpie is going to be there for you.

Since the day I opened up shop nine years ago, Baby Bea (my daughter Brinley) has gained a sister, Cara, and my hair has gone gray. But people still love the warm, relaxing nature of comfort food—and the Comfort Diner is still here to serve it.

Now with *The Comfort Diner Cookbook,* you've got everything you need to create the same experience at home (save for the neon lights). This book is designed to make your cooking life easy and your family happy. The recipes don't include hard-to-find ingredients. In fact, most of the dishes can be made with ingredients that (if they're not in your pantry already) are carried by most supermarkets. The techniques and methods definitely do not require a degree in culinary arts to perfect. And you can always substitute an ingredient or adapt the recipe to your liking. So have a good time with it. This is meant to be a book of recipes that you'll use day in and day out. It's not a coffee table book. Go ahead: spill pancake batter on the pages, singe the corners, crack the binding so the book flops open to your favorite recipe. Nothing could please me more. (Well, maybe winning a Scrabble tournament would please me more than seeing your beat-up copy of this book, but you know what I mean.)

Go forth and comfort!

"Can I get extra syrup?"

chapter 1

big breakfasts

Start Your Day the Right Way

There's nothing quite like the buzz of a diner during breakfast. Every inch of the grill is packed with pancakes, eggs, and bacon. Thick batter hits the waffle iron with a loud sizzle, sending up the heady smell of hot butter. The coffee urns are brewing nonstop to fill the bottomless mugs. The wait staff is running at top speed, plunking down plates at tables and making sure the Lemon Ricotta Pancakes don't end up going to the guy who ordered the White Sausage Gravy and Biscuits. It's a whirlwind of activity, and a feast for the senses.

At home, you may be cooking for yourself, a few guests, or a whole houseful of people, but no matter what, serving a memorable breakfast is a way of starting the day with glorious promise. There's something supremely comforting in a warm stack of buttermilk pancakes—made from scratch, soaking up the butter and maple syrup—or an enormous slice of French toast, overstuffed with fresh blueberries and strawberries. After feasting on food like this, all is right with the world—mainly because there's nothing you can do but take a nap immediately afterward. And that's okay. When you wake up, that glorious promise of the day ahead will still be there. You just might have to take advantage of it tomorrow!

buttermilk pancakes

Serves 6

Let me just warn you: you're about to spoil yourself and your family. It's so hard to go back to boxed pancake mixes after making these from scratch. And look, if you're going to make pancakes anyway, you might as well do it right. Our pancakes were voted the best in New York City by a readers' poll in *Time Out New York*. So go ahead — impress your friends and neighbors when they ask, "How was your weekend?" You can reply, "Oh, I just whipped up pancakes from scratch — the best pancakes in New York City, thank you very much!"

This is a basic recipe for pancakes, but if you like some fruit in the mix — maybe blueberries, strawberries, or bananas — you have two options. You can start to cook the pancake, then add a handful of fruit into the batter. Or you can cook the pancakes plain, and top with fresh fruit. Either way, they're sure to please.

½ cup (1 stick) unsalted butter

2 cups all-purpose flour

1 tablespoon plus 1 teaspoon sugar

1 teaspoon salt

1 teaspoon baking powder

½ teaspoon baking soda

½ cup whole milk

1½ cups buttermilk

2 large eggs

1. In a small saucepan, melt ¼ cup of the butter and set it aside to cool.

2. In a large bowl, mix the flour, sugar, salt, baking powder, and baking soda.

3. In a separate bowl combine the milk and buttermilk. Whisk in the eggs. Slowly add the ¼ cup melted butter to the eggs. (Be sure that the butter has cooled. If the butter is too warm, it will cook the eggs.) Whisk to combine.

4. Add the wet ingredients to the dry ingredients and whisk until just mixed.

5. On a griddle or in a nonstick skillet, melt 1 tablespoon of the butter over medium heat. Scoop ¼ to ½ cup of the batter onto the surface and cook for about 1 minute, or until small air holes appear on the pancake's surface. Flip the pancake and cook for 1 minute more, until cooked through. Repeat to make the remaining pancakes, adding more butter to the pan as needed.

the great pumpkin pancakes

Serves 6 to 8

You'll be surprised how much these pancakes taste like warm pumpkin pie. Make them around Halloween and have a little fun: cut up some fruit and make scary (or happy) faces on top. These are moist, flavorful, and way more of a treat than regular pancakes.

¾ cup unsalted butter
  (1½ sticks)

1½ cups all-purpose flour

½ cup cornmeal

¼ cup plus 1 tablespoon sugar

1 tablespoon baking powder

1 teaspoon salt

2 teaspoons powdered ginger

2 teaspoons cinnamon

Pinch of ground clove (from
  1 clove)

Pinch of ground allspice

2 large eggs

1 cup canned pumpkin puree

1¾ cups whole milk

1. In a small saucepan, melt ½ cup of the butter and set it aside to cool.

2. In a large bowl, mix the flour, cornmeal, sugar, baking powder, salt, ginger, cinnamon, clove, and allspice, then sift to combine thoroughly.

3. In a separate mixing bowl, beat the eggs and mix in the pumpkin puree. Blend thoroughly with a wooden spoon until smooth and combined. Slowly add the cooled butter. (Be sure it has cooled. If the butter is too warm, it will cook the eggs.) Add the milk.

4. Add the pumpkin mixture to the dry ingredients and stir until just mixed.

5. On a griddle or in a nonstick skillet, melt 1 tablespoon of the butter over medium heat. Scoop ¼ to ½ cup of batter onto the surface and cook for about 1 minute, or until small air holes appear on the surface of the pancake. Flip the pancake and cook for 1 minute more, until cooked through. Repeat to cook the remaining pancakes, adding more butter to the pan as needed.

gingerbread pancakes

If you like gingerbread cookies, really soft ones, you're gonna love gingerbread pancakes. They're really great on a winter's morning when the smell wafts through the house. There are a lot of ingredients here, but measuring out each one is well worth it.

¾ cup unsalted butter (1½ sticks)

2 cups all-purpose flour

½ cup plus 2 tablespoons brown sugar

1 tablespoon baking powder

1½ teaspoons baking soda

¼ teaspoon salt

1 tablespoon powdered ginger

½ tablespoon ground cinnamon

⅛ teaspoon ground cloves (from 2 cloves)

Pinch of nutmeg

2 large eggs

2 tablespoons molasses

1½ cups whole milk

½ cup sour cream

1. In a small saucepan, melt ½ cup of the butter and set it aside to cool.

2. In a large bowl, combine the flour, brown sugar, baking powder, baking soda, salt, ginger, cinnamon, cloves, and nutmeg until well blended.

3. In a separate bowl, beat the eggs lightly. Stir in the molasses, cooled butter, and milk. Fold in the sour cream.

4. Pour the wet ingredients into the flour mixture and stir until all the lumps are removed.

5. On a griddle or in a nonstick skillet, melt 1 tablespoon of the butter over medium heat. Scoop ¼ to ½ cup of batter onto the surface and cook for about 1 minute, or until small air holes appear on the surface of the pancake. Flip the pancake and cook for 1 minute more, until cooked through. Repeat to cook the remaining pancakes, adding more butter to the pan as needed.

lemon ricotta pancakes

Serves 4

These pancakes are so light and elegant, they almost seem too classy for a diner. Almost! They're a bit like French crepes, but never fear — they're still proper pancakes and very easy to make. These are just heaven with some fresh raspberries on top.

½ cup (1 stick) unsalted butter

4 large eggs

1 cup ricotta cheese

½ teaspoon vanilla extract

2 tablespoons grated lemon zest

3 tablespoons lemon juice

2 tablespoons granulated sugar

½ cup plus 1 tablespoon flour

Confectioners' sugar, to serve

1. In a small saucepan, melt ¼ cup of the butter. Allow it to cool.

2. In a large bowl, beat the eggs, then add the ricotta, vanilla, lemon zest, and lemon juice. Add the sugar and whisk thoroughly. Slowly add the melted butter and continue to mix. Add all of the flour and mix thoroughly.

3. On a griddle or in a nonstick skillet, melt 1 tablespoon of the butter over medium heat. Scoop ¼ to ½ cup of batter onto the surface and cook for about 1 minute, or until small air holes appear on the pancake's surface. Flip the pancake and cook for 1 minute more, until cooked through. Repeat to cook the remaining pancakes, adding more butter to the pan as needed.

4. Serve with confectioners' sugar sprinkled on top.

big bread french toast

When we say "big," we mean it. Our French toast starts with three-inch-wide pieces of bread. So when people see our French toast for the first time, their eyes get as big as the slices on the plate. If you can't find sweet brioche bread, an eggy challah bread will work, but be sure that the slices are thick and even.

And don't stop at just plain French toast. We've included two variations on the regular version: berry stuffed and banana nutty. And you'd be a nut not to try 'em!

2 tablespoons ground cinnamon

3 large eggs

1½ cups heavy cream

1½ cups whole milk

¼ cup confectioners' sugar

1 teaspoon vanilla extract

¼ cup (½ stick) unsalted butter

1 loaf brioche bread, unsliced

Maple syrup, to serve

1. In a large bowl, combine the cinnamon with the eggs, cream, milk, sugar, and vanilla, whisking thoroughly after each addition so that the cinnamon is fully moistened. This will prevent it from floating on the top of the batter.

2. Preheat a griddle or sauté pan to medium-high heat and melt 1 tablespoon of the butter.

3. Slice the bread into four 3-inch-wide slices. Halve each piece of bread on the diagonal, as you would a sandwich. Dip the triangles of bread into the batter and place immediately on the hot griddle or pan.

4. Cook each side for 1 to 2 minutes. Flip the bread so that the sliced middle portion is on the heat and cook for about 1 minute. Repeat to cook the remaining slices, adding more butter to the pan as needed. Serve hot with maple syrup.

berry-stuffed french toast

½ cup blueberries, roughly chopped

8 strawberries, sliced

After step 3 above: In a small bowl, mix together the blueberries and strawberries. Hold each triangle of bread with the right angle in your hand. From the flat, diagonally sliced side, scoop out a hole that is about 1 inch deep. The hole should be just deep and wide enough to fit the berries without having them fall out. Stuff an equal portion of the berries into each slice. Continue with step 4.

banana nutty-stuffed french toast

4 bananas, sliced

2 tablespoons chopped walnuts

After step 3 above: In a bowl, mix the bananas and nuts. Hold each triangle of bread with the right angle in your hand. From the flat, diagonally sliced side, scoop out a hole that is about 1 inch deep. The hole should be just deep and wide enough to fit the filling without having it fall out. Stuff an equal portion of bananas and nuts into each slice. Continue with step 4.

white sausage gravy
and biscuits

Serves 4

One Sunday morning, I had some friends over for breakfast and made them this hearty dish. On Monday afternoon, I got a call from one of them begging to come over for leftovers at dinnertime: "I was thinking about that gravy all day!" he said. That's what this breakfast does to people — sticks to their ribs and in their heads. Serve this gravy with our Buttermilk Biscuits and you'll have friends for life.

1 pound breakfast sausage meat (or 20 to 25 small breakfast sausage links, casings removed)

¼ cup (½ stick) unsalted butter

¼ cup all-purpose flour

3 cups whole milk

Salt and freshly ground black pepper to taste

Pinch of nutmeg

Buttermilk Biscuits (page 38)

1. In a tall-sided saucepan at medium-high heat, cook the sausage for about 5 minutes, until the meat is cooked through. Remove the sausage and set it aside.

2. Without draining the fat from the pan, add the butter and melt it over low heat. Mix in the flour and stir to combine thoroughly. Heat for 3 to 4 minutes, until thick.

3. Pour the milk into the pan. Increase the heat and bring the milk to a boil, stirring. Reduce the heat to medium and simmer for 20 minutes, stirring often. The gravy should be thick and creamy. Season with salt, pepper, and nutmeg.

4. Crumble the cooked sausage into the gravy and serve with Buttermilk Biscuits.

White Sausage Gravy and Biscuits is a breakfast for a hearty — very hearty — appetite. It's a staple of southern cuisine but can be found at diners all over, especially in the Midwest. It's the sort of meal to have before a major physical chore — like rustling up the cattle, raising a barn, or, well, mowing the lawn.

When you're shopping for ingredients, be sure to note that you'll need "breakfast sausage," which is typically simpler and sweeter than other types of sausage. Whereas Italian sausage tends to be flavored with herbs and spices such as oregano and fennel, breakfast sausage can be flavored with maple syrup or brown sugar. As long as the sausage is made with just a mild mix of spices or a sweetener, it can blend well with the creamy gravy. So if you're craving that gourmet chicken-and-black-truffle sausage, remember: patience is a virtue. Save it for dinner.

breakfast burrito

Sometimes you just aren't awake enough to bother with a knife and fork. And for those times, there's the breakfast burrito. This grab-and-go package conceals a truckload of food inside. Pick this up with your hands, and you'll feel the heft of two kinds of cheese, avocado, black beans, and eggs. It's filling all right, and has plenty of zesty Mexican flavor to wake you right up.

4 12-inch flour tortillas

8 large eggs

3 tablespoons unsalted butter

2 avocados, peeled, pitted, and sliced in eighths

1 cup canned black beans, drained (from 1 16-ounce can)

1 cup (4 ounces) shredded Cheddar cheese

1 cup (4 ounces) shredded pepper jack cheese

½ cup Lively Tomato Salsa (page 121)

1. Preheat the oven to its lowest setting. Wrap the tortillas in aluminum foil and place them in the oven.

2. In a bowl, beat the eggs lightly. In a nonstick skillet, melt the butter over medium heat. Pour the eggs into the pan and scramble them gently. Cook until the eggs are set as you like them.

3. To assemble each burrito: Place a warm tortilla on a clean, flat surface. Place one fourth of the eggs horizontally across the center of the tortilla. Add 4 slices of avocado, ¼ cup of black beans, ¼ cup of Cheddar, ¼ cup of pepper jack, and 2 tablespoons of salsa.

4. Fold the sides, about 1 inch, of the tortilla inward. Pick up the edge closest to you and roll it over the ingredients. Tuck under the ingredients. Roll the tortilla over so that it is firmly closed. Slice in half and serve.

Want to teach your kids a lesson about the four food groups?

Try making the Breakfast Burrito with them. It's a complete meal with a little bit of everything rolled up inside. If you don't count eggs as meat, you can add some spicy chorizo sausage to the mix for a protein-packed breakfast.

Though burritos typically include the staples of Mexican food, they're considered more of a Mexican-American development and are said to have originated in the southwestern United States. A Breakfast Burrito is a close cousin to the more traditional Huevos Rancheros, literally "rancher's eggs" or "ranch-style" eggs, which consists of eggs and salsa (plus lots of toppings when served the Comfort Diner way) served on a fried corn tortilla. Both the Breakfast Burrito and Huevos Rancheros are a great reason to keep a bowl of our Lively Tomato Salsa on hand at all times. In a matter of minutes, you can have a hearty egg breakfast — whether you've got corn or flour tortillas around — enlivened with your own homemade salsa.

three-cheese omelet

It's just a fact. People love cheese. Maybe that's why this omelet is so popular. And if you really love cheese — which puts you in the same supercheesy league as me — go on and add a fourth cheese. Just don't expect to run a marathon in the afternoon. This recipe serves one because it's best to make omelets individually.

When it comes to serving omelets, I have the same philosophy as I do about serving hamburgers. I could list all the wacky combinations for you. Or you could decide what you like best and toss it all in. That's why at the Comfort Diner, we offer the Imagination Omelet: it lets you be the star. So use this recipe (with or without the cheese), as a place to start. You could use ingredients suggested as hamburger toppings (see page 67) or throw in whatever you like. Just make sure that the portions aren't so huge that you can't close your creation!

1 tablespoon unsalted butter

3 large eggs

Pinch of salt

$\frac{1}{8}$ teaspoon freshly ground black pepper to taste

2 tablespoons shredded Cheddar cheese

1 tablespoon shredded Swiss cheese

1 tablespoon shredded pepper jack cheese

1. In a nonstick skillet or omelet pan, melt the butter over medium-high heat.

2. In a small bowl, beat the eggs. Season them lightly with salt and pepper. Pour the eggs into the pan. Heat for 1 minute. Using a spatula, scrape the eggs away from the pan edges. Tilt the pan and allow the liquidy egg from the top to trickle down and fill the space.

3. Heat for 1 to 2 minutes more, or until the eggs are set as you like them. Sprinkle the Cheddar, Swiss, and pepper jack cheeses on half of the omelet. Heat for about 1 minute more, until the cheese has melted slightly.

4. To fold the omelet, loosen it and tip the pan so that the cheeseless side of the omelet is against the side of the pan. Using a spatula to help, fold the cheeseless side of the omelet onto the other half, making a half-moon shape. Continue to cook for 1 minute or less, depending on your preference. Serve right away.

The Ultimate Host Breakfast

When you have houseguests, it's always a treat for them to wake up to the smell of fresh-baked blueberry muffins and brewing coffee. If you've got light eaters in town, muffins and fruit will be plenty, but you'll be the hostess with the mostest if you offer individual omelets, too.

Blueberry Muffins (page 149)

Three-Cheese Omelets (page 24)

Fresh fruit salad

Diner Trivia

Rough and tumble diners weren't always a friendly place for the ladies. But owners realized they could make more money if they convinced women that diners weren't for men only. Signs bearing the words LADIES INVITED started appearing in the 1920s, along with dainty touches like flower boxes and frosted glass, and booths where women could sit if they weren't keen to sit on stools at the counter.

huevos rancheros

The Comfort Diner staff members — many of whom are from Mexico — whip up a version of this dish for themselves all the time. After I tasted it, I knew it had to be on the menu — it's a diner classic in the making. The crispy tortilla contrasts with the soft eggs and smooth cheese just right. This recipe gives you the directions for fried eggs, but you can make them any way you like — we certainly let the customers be the boss on that one. And if you get hooked, make this for lunch, too — just skip the eggs and throw some grilled chicken on instead.

1/4 cup vegetable oil

4 corn tortillas

1 cup canned black beans, drained (from 1 16-ounce can)

4 tablespoons unsalted butter

8 large eggs

1/8 teaspoon salt

1/8 teaspoon freshly ground black pepper

1 cup (4 ounces) shredded Cheddar cheese

1 cup (4 ounces) shredded pepper jack cheese

1/2 cup Lively Tomato Salsa (page 121)

1/2 cup sour cream

1. Preheat the broiler or oven to 300° F. In a nonstick skillet, heat 2 tablespoons of the oil over medium heat. When the oil is hot, fry the tortillas for 2 to 3 minutes each, flipping after 1 minute, until crispy. If extra oil is needed for remaining tortillas, pour more into the pan. Set each tortilla aside until all are cooked.

2. In a saucepan, warm the black beans over medium heat for 4 minutes, until the beans are warmed through, and set aside.

3. Pour out any remaining oil from the skillet and return it to the burner.

4. For each serving of fried eggs: In the same skillet, heat 1 tablespoon of the butter over medium-high heat. Break 2 eggs into the pan and allow them to cook for 2 minutes undisturbed, or if you like eggs cooked on both sides, flip after 1 minute. Season the eggs with salt and pepper as they cook.

5. To assemble: Place a fried tortilla on each plate. Top with 2 eggs, then 1/4 cup of Cheddar and 1/4 cup of pepper jack cheese. Sprinkle 1/4 cup of beans on top, then dot with 2 tablespoons of salsa and 2 tablespoons of sour cream. Serve right away.

red flannel hash

Red Flannel Hash is an old New England dish that evolved from the leftovers after a boiled dinner of corned beef and potatoes. There are no hard and fast rules about what goes into Red Flannel Hash. No matter what you mix into the dinner, you can chop it up and enjoy it for breakfast. Well, there is one rule. If you're making this hash for breakfast (and not just using leftovers), don't add the beets until the last minute. If you mix them in too early, everything will turn red — you won't be able to tell a beet from a sweet potato from an Idaho potato. And that will give you Very *Very* Red Flannel Hash.

2 Idaho potatoes (unpeeled)

2 sweet potatoes (unpeeled)

4 beets (unpeeled)

3 tablespoons vegetable oil

2 cups chopped Spanish or white onions (2 medium-sized onions)

3 tablespoons Worcestershire sauce

Salt and freshly ground black pepper to taste

1 pound precooked corned beef, chopped

4 finely chopped scallions (green and white parts)

1. Fill two large pots with cold water. In one, place the Idaho and sweet potatoes. In the other, place the beets. Bring both to a boil. Allow the potatoes to cook for 30 to 40 minutes, until tender. Be careful not to overcook. Allow the beets to cook for about 45 minutes, until tender.

2. Drain and peel the potatoes and beets. Chop into 1-inch dice.

3. In a large pan, heat the oil over medium heat. Sauté the onions for 5 minutes, until soft. Add the Worcestershire sauce and continue cooking for 2 minutes more. Season with salt and black pepper.

4. Add the beef and heat for 3 minutes. Add the potatoes and scallions and heat for 3 minutes more, until warm. Toss in the cooked beets and heat for 2 minutes. Adjust seasoning.

"Just a little something"

chapter 2

small plates

The Right Bite at the Right Time

What exactly are "Small Plates"? They're those smaller servings of food that satisfy you when you're not quite hungry enough for a real meal. They're what you need when you look aimlessly in the fridge for just a little nosh, but something more than a bag of pretzels. They're what you wish for at the office around 4:00 p.m., and they're what you want when you come home at midnight after a party. That's when a bowl of Grandma's Chicken Soup or a chunk of Jalapeño Cheddar Cornbread (or both!) would come in handy. When you get that twinge of in-between hunger, wouldn't it be a dream to have just a few Buffalo Wings? How about a crispy Potato Pancake?

In this chapter are recipes you can make with ease, then eat right away or slip into the refrigerator. When your crew is lookin' in the kitchen for chow, they'll find a surprise—and they'll get to experience the Comfort Diner motto firsthand: Time to eat good food. So no matter when it's time to nibble, graze, or munch, the good stuff will be at the ready. (And so will a few hugs of appreciation, too.) Of course, these dishes make terrific appetizers or light lunches as well.

potato pancakes

Makes 12 to 15 pancakes

Everybody says it, but I mean it: my grandmother made the best potato pancakes. Crunchy on the outside and soft on the inside, with a little sour cream and apple-sauce, they were sheer delight. At the restaurant, we can make them extra crunchy by dipping them in the fryer. At home, it's easier to make them on a griddle or in a skillet. What you might lose in crunch, you'll make up for in flavor. The pan-cakes' special ingredient, mushrooms, have a much stronger presence when the potato pancakes are sautéed rather than fried.

4 cups shredded Idaho potatoes (2 to 3 potatoes)

2 cups shredded Spanish onions (2 medium onions)

2½ cups thinly sliced, stemmed shiitake mushrooms (or other variety; 12 to 14 mushrooms)

2 large eggs

1 cup all-purpose flour

1 teaspoon salt

1 teaspoon freshly ground black pepper

6 tablespoons unsalted butter

Thick-N-Chunky Applesauce (page 110), to serve

1. In a large bowl, combine the potatoes, onions, and mushrooms.

2. In a small bowl, beat the eggs, then add them to the vegetables. Mix in the flour to combine. Season with the salt and pepper.

3. In a nonstick skillet over medium-high heat or a griddle at 300°F, melt 2 tablespoons of the butter. Scoop up ¼ cup of the potato batter and wring out the excess liquid with your hands. (Do this over the sink or an empty bowl.) Flatten it into a 3-inch round pancake. Place the pancake in the skillet and sauté for 6 to 7 minutes on each side, until golden brown. You can sauté several pancakes at the same time, but allow at least 1 inch of space between them. Repeat until there is no batter remaining, adding additional butter to the skillet as needed. Serve with Thick-N-Chunky Applesauce.

What's the difference between a potato pancake and a latke?

Well, the difference lies not so much in ingredients or tastes as in symbolism. Latkes are potato pancakes, often served during the Jewish holiday of Hanukkah. The grated potato-and-onion pattie is cooked in oil, which symbolizes the oil in the biblical story of the Macabees. After years of fighting, they reclaimed the Holy Temple of Jerusalem. After they had cleaned the ravaged temple, they had only enough oil to keep the eternal flame that burns in all Jewish houses of worship alight for one night. But a miracle occurred and the oil burned on for eight nights.

Some will argue that latkes include matzo meal as a binder, whereas regular potato pancakes typically do not. But in general, the ingredients are pretty much standard: grated potatoes, onion, egg, flour, and salt and pepper. Still, if you're looking for a rule that defines the difference, here's one: all latkes are potato pancakes, but not all potato pancakes are latkes.

Diner Trivia

"Blue Plate Special"

While most restaurants have daily specials, the early diner specials were served on blue plates that were divided into three sections for the meat, potato, and vegetable. That meant there were fewer dishes to wash. And that cost savings was passed on to the customer in the form of a low-priced meal.

buffalo wings

Serves 4 as a meal, 6 to 8 as appetizers

When it comes to Buffalo wings, I'm a wimp. I can have only about three before I can't feel my lips anymore. So when I set out to make a sauce for my wings, I made sure it was the right kind of spicy — which for me means not too hot. Be sure to take the time to make our blue cheese dressing. It's cool, rich, and creamy — just the thing to balance the wings. And if you have some extra dressing, you can make yourself a salad.

½ cup (1 stick) unsalted butter, melted

2 cups hot sauce

1 canned chipotle pepper, finely chopped

3 tablespoons honey

2 tablespoons Worcestershire sauce

2 tablespoons A-1 steak sauce

1 cup all-purpose flour

1 tablespoon salt

1 tablespoon freshly ground black pepper

24 whole chicken wings (or 48 already jointed wing pieces)

1 cup vegetable oil

To serve

4 carrots, cut into sticks

4 stalks celery, cut into sticks

Blue Cheese Dressing (page 129)

1. Preheat the oven to 250°F. Pour the melted butter, hot sauce, chipotle, honey, Worcestershire, and steak sauce into a blender and mix until smooth. In a large saucepan over low heat, warm the sauce until simmering. Meanwhile, in a medium bowl, combine the flour, salt, and pepper.

2. If using whole wings: with a sharp knife, cut each wing at the joints into three pieces. Discard the wing tips. Coat the wings with the flour mixture and shake off any excess.

3. In a deep stockpot, heat ½ cup of the oil over medium heat to 375°F, or until the oil sizzles when a wing is dipped in it. Add as many wings as will fit into the pot without crowding. Fry the wings, flipping occasionally, for 10 to 12 minutes, until golden brown and cooked through on all sides. Blot the cooked wings on paper towels, then place them in a baking dish or tray in the oven and finish cooking the remaining wings, using the remaining oil if needed.

4. When all the wings are cooked, remove them from the oven, place them into a large mixing bowl, and pour the warm sauce over them. Toss gently until evenly coated. Serve with the carrots, celery, and Blue Cheese Dressing.

Buffalo wings are the ultimate sports-bar snack. Really, is a football game even worth watching if you don't have a bucket of hot wings to gnaw on? These American munchies were born in 1964 at the Anchor Bar in Buffalo, New York. The bartender's mother, Teressa Bellissimo, wanted to feed some hungry customers, so she deep-fried a batch of chicken wings and tossed them in a special hot sauce that she created on the spot. She served the bar's house dressing — blue cheese — on the side. And the rest is history. The treats were an instant hit; people flocked to the bar after hearing about the wings, and the concept spread far and wide. So much so that Buffalo wings are a must-have on the menu of any sports bar worth its salt in this country. And Teressa's innovation did not go unrewarded: the Anchor Bar has since received a James Beard Foundation "American Classics" Award.

chicken skewers with honey mustard dressing

Serves 6

If you need a healthful, kid-friendly alternative to fried chicken fingers, this is it. There's just a little garlic on the chicken — and you don't even have to use that, if you'd rather not. The Honey Mustard Dressing can also be made sweeter, if you like.

4 6- to 8-ounce chicken breasts

3 garlic cloves, minced

¼ cup olive oil

¼ teaspoon salt

¼ teaspoon freshly ground black pepper

Honey Mustard Dressing (page 120)

1. Place the chicken breasts between 2 sheets of waxed paper and pound to an even thickness. Slice into long, 2-inch-wide strips. Place the chicken strips in a baking dish and toss with the garlic and oil. Marinate for at least 30 minutes. Meanwhile, soak bamboo skewers in water for 10 minutes. (This will prevent the skewers from splintering.)

2. Season the chicken with salt and pepper. Thread the chicken onto the skewers.

3. In a grill pan over medium heat, lay the skewers flat and cook the chicken for about 5 minutes per side, until cooked through. (Alternatively, preheat the oven to 350°F. Place the chicken skewers in a baking dish and cook for 10 minutes, until cooked through.) Serve on the skewers with Honey Mustard Dressing as a dip.

grandma's chicken soup

What's the best comfort when you're sick? Chicken soup. What do you want when you're feeling blue? Chicken soup. What do you crave when you're celebrating good news? Well, probably champagne, but then the next day, maybe you'll need some chicken soup. We use a whole chicken to get all the flavor, fat, and lots of chicken meat. There aren't a lot of fancy ingredients to complicate things: just the essentials.

1 whole chicken (about 3½ pounds)

½ bunch fresh thyme

½ cup olive oil

2 cups small-diced Spanish onions
(2 medium-sized onions)

2 cups small-diced carrots (2 to 3 medium-sized carrots)

1 cup small-diced celery (3 stalks)

¼ teaspoon salt

¼ teaspoon freshly ground black pepper

½ pound spaghetti

1. In a large stock pot, bring a gallon of water to a boil. Add the chicken and thyme. Simmer gently for 30 to 40 minutes.

2. Meanwhile, in a sauté pan, heat the oil over medium-high heat. Sauté the onions, carrots, and celery until just soft, about 5 minutes.

3. When the chicken has finished cooking (the breast meat should be white rather than pink, and the drumsticks should move easily when jiggled), remove it from the pot. Allow to cool slightly. Meanwhile, strain the chicken's cooking liquid and return it to the pot. Add the sautéed vegetables.

4. Remove the meat from the chicken. Discard the bones and add the meat to the pot. Return to a boil, then simmer for 10 minutes. Season with the salt and pepper.

5. Meanwhile, bring a separate pot of water to a boil. Break the pasta into small pieces and cook according to package directions. Add it to the chicken soup just before serving. If you plan to serve the soup later, do not add the pasta until ready to serve.

chilled tomato soup

Sometimes it gets so hot and humid in the summer that the only way to cool down is with a bowl of chilled soup. This one does the trick, though you will have to turn on the oven to roast the tomatoes. But, hey, it takes only half an hour to turn raw tomatoes into sweet, roasted goodness. They're worth it. Just crank up that air-conditioning.

6 fresh plum tomatoes, halved lengthwise

3 tablespoons olive oil

½ cup small-diced shallots (about 3 shallots)

2 garlic cloves, minced

2 cups small-diced Idaho potato, peeled (1 to 2 potatoes)

1 cup small-diced celery (2 to 3 stalks)

1 bunch fresh basil

1 cup canned plum tomatoes

1 tablespoon salt, or to taste

½ tablespoon freshly ground black pepper

¼ cup water (or liquid from roasted tomatoes)

1. Preheat the oven to 350°F. In a large baking dish, place the fresh tomatoes flat side down. Roast in the oven for 30 minutes. Remove the tomatoes from the oven and allow them to cool for 15 minutes. Peel off and discard the skins; place the tomatoes in a large bowl.

2. In a saucepan, heat the olive oil over medium heat. Sauté the shallots, garlic, potato, and celery for about 5 minutes, until soft.

3. To the bowl containing the oven-roasted tomatoes, add the sautéed vegetables, ¼ cup whole basil leaves, and the canned tomatoes. Toss lightly, then pour into a blender or food processor. Blend until chunky but well mixed. Add the salt, pepper, water or liquid from the roasted tomatoes, and blend again until combined.

4. Chill for at least 2 hours before serving. Adjust seasoning to taste, ladle into bowls, and decorate each bowl with basil leaves.

jalapeño cheddar cornbread

Serves 8 to 10

Forget the grainy, bland cornbread you find in supermarkets. This sweet, moist cornbread has a gentle kick from the jalapeños and a toothsome feel from the fresh corn. This recipe will make you the star of the potluck, and it won't keep you at the hot stove all day. (But go ahead and say it did anyway!)

2 cups fresh corn kernels
  (from 3 ears of corn)

1½ cups cornmeal

2 cups all-purpose flour

1 tablespoon baking powder

2 teaspoons baking soda

½ cup sugar

3 large eggs

2 cups whole milk

1 tablespoon vanilla extract

2 tablespoons olive oil

¼ cup (½ stick) unsalted
  butter, melted and cooled

1 cup plus 2 tablespoons
  (5 ounces) shredded
  Cheddar cheese

1 jalapeño pepper, minced

1. Preheat the oven to 350°F. Grease a 9×12-inch baking dish. In a saucepan, combine the corn kernels with ½ cup of water. Bring to a boil. Reduce the heat and simmer for 3 minutes. Discard the water and set aside the corn.

2. In a large bowl, mix the cornmeal, flour, baking powder, baking soda, and sugar. In a separate bowl, mix the eggs, milk, vanilla, and olive oil. Add the melted butter slowly.

3. Pour the wet ingredients into the dry ingredients. Mix gently, then add 1 cup of the Cheddar and all of the jalapeño and the simmered corn.

4. Pour the mixture into the baking dish. Sprinkle the remaining Cheddar over the top. Bake for 30 to 35 minutes, until the cornbread is firm and a toothpick inserted at the center comes out clean.

buttermilk biscuits

Makes 12 to 14 biscuits

I know the recipe says it makes twelve to fourteen biscuits, but it never did for me. Maybe that's because I always seemed to eat at least two or three before they could cool off. Put a pat of butter on, watch it start to melt, pop it in your mouth, and you'll be planning your next batch.

4 cups all-purpose flour

2 tablespoons baking powder

¼ cup sugar

½ cup heavy cream

½ cup buttermilk

½ teaspoon vanilla extract

½ cup (1 stick) unsalted butter, melted and cooled

1. Preheat the oven to 350°F. In a large bowl, mix the flour, baking powder, and sugar. In a separate bowl, mix the heavy cream, buttermilk, vanilla, and butter.

2. Pour the wet ingredients into the dry ingredients and mix until just combined. Turn the dough onto a floured surface. Roll the dough out to a ½-inch thickness. (Do not handle the dough more than is necessary to gather it into a ball and roll it out.)

3. Using a 2-inch round cookie cutter or small drinking glass, cut the dough into circles. Place them on a greased cookie sheet, or one lined with parchment, or an ovenproof baking mat.

4. Bake for 15 to 18 minutes, until cooked through and lightly golden.

Time to Refresh

For a light brunch on a hot summer day, the best way to go is with cold, fresh ingredients. To avoid cooking a lot in the day, roast the tomatoes the night before, then whip up the soup in the morning. The cornbread, too, can be made ahead.

Chilled Tomato Soup (page 36)

Jalapeño Cheddar Cornbread (page 37)

Chinese Chicken Salad (page 49)

rhode island clam fritters

Serves 6 to 8

Near my hometown of Bristol, Rhode Island, there was an amusement park called Rocky Point. Sure, the rides were fun, but the fried clam cakes were unbelievable. For the restaurant, I made these smaller and called them clam fritters — so there wouldn't be any confusion with crab cakes. But you can call these delicious morsels anything you want. Don't be put off by frying at home — these will satisfy even your most jaded thrill seekers.

¾ cup all-purpose flour

1½ tablespoons baking powder

3 tablespoons chopped chives

1 teaspoon Cajun spice mix (or Old Bay Seasoning)

1 teaspoon garlic powder

2 cups raw shucked clams, halved

3 large eggs

¼ teaspoon salt

¼ teaspoon freshly ground black pepper

2 cups vegetable oil

Your Very Own Tartar Sauce (page 123) or Tangy Remoulade Sauce (page 124), to serve

1. In a large bowl, mix the flour, baking powder, chives, Cajun spice mix, and garlic powder. Add the clams and eggs. Mix until the clams are distributed evenly. Season with the salt and pepper.

2. Form the mixture into small balls, about 2 teaspoons in each.

3. Heat the oil in a large pot over medium-high heat. Fry 1 ball in the oil for 1 to 2 minutes, until crispy and cooked thorough. Test for doneness. Continue to make the balls and fry as many of them as will fit in the pot without crowding. The fritters should not touch each other. Place the cooked fritters on paper towels to drain excess oil.

4. Serve with Your Very Own Tartar Sauce or Tangy Remoulade Sauce.

Big Party, Small Bites

Finger food at a party is always a hit. And if you're serving cocktails, it's a must. For a group of eight to ten, one recipe of each of the following will make for hearty hors d'oeuvres. For a larger group, you can double or triple the quantities.

Chicken Skewers with Honey Mustard Dressing (page 34)

Shrimp with Bloody Mary Cocktail Sauce (page 41)

Trio Tuna Salad on crackers (page 45)

Lively Tomato Salsa with chips (page 121)

Chilled Tomato Soup (page 36) served in shot glasses

Diner Trivia

Diner cooks have a wide variety of ways to call in your sandwich order. "High and dry" means without butter, mayo, or lettuce. With "Rabbit Food" gets you lettuce on the sandwich, but "Hold the Grass" keeps it out. If you wanted your tuna on toast, you'll get it "on down," which refers to the action of pressing down the toaster button. To "pin a rose on it" adds an onion to an order.

shrimp with bloody mary cocktail sauce

I like shrimp, but I love a good Bloody Mary. One day I had an idea about how to combine the two. After all, the ingredients that go into the famous cocktail aren't really all that different from a cocktail sauce. So I turned into a mad scientist, mixing ingredients together until I hit on the perfect concoction. Don't feel restricted by this recipe — it's just the starting point. Add more Tabasco or horseradish if you want more kick. Add more ketchup if you want it sweeter. Get creative and suit yourself!

16 large shrimp, peeled and cleaned

¼ cup plus 2 tablespoons tomato juice

3 tablespoons vodka

⅓ cup prepared horseradish

¼ cup ketchup

1 tablespoon Worcestershire sauce

1 teaspoon Tabasco sauce

1 teaspoon minced garlic

Salt and freshly ground pepper to taste

1. Bring a large pot of water to a boil. Add the shrimp and boil for 1 to 2 minutes, until shrimp are opaque and cooked through.

2. In a medium bowl, mix the tomato juice, vodka, and horseradish. Add the ketchup, Worcestershire sauce, Tabasco sauce, and garlic. Whisk to fully combine. Season with salt and pepper, if needed.

3. Serve the shrimp warm or cold, with the sauce on the side.

"I'll have the Cobb."

chapter 3

scrumptious salads

Diner Food Is Healthy, Too

At the Comfort Diner, a salad can mean anything from a big bowl of leafy greens topped with refreshing vegetables to a heaping scoop of creamy egg salad served on a bed of crisp lettuce. Either way, we know there's no reason why you can't eat healthfully at a diner—and there's every reason to eat right at home.

That's why this chapter is packed with salads for every taste and appetite. For meat-eaters, for example, there's the Warm Taco Salad. For vegetarians, there's the Chopped Health Salad. For those who want the taste of the classics (just slightly updated), there is the Ultimate Diner-Salad Trio of egg, chicken, and tuna salads.

What's fun—and yes, salads can be fun—about these recipes is that they offer some versatility. The Comfort Diner Grilled Chicken Salad can be served in a big bowl or plated beautifully on four dishes. It can start or make a meal. Leave off the chicken, and it is a colorful side salad. It's all up to you.

Regardless of how you serve them, these salads are designed to make vegetables taste great—and that goes for die-hard, meat-and-potatoes types as well as longtime light eaters suffering from salad fatigue. Boring salads begone!

the ultimate diner-salad trio

When it comes to diner salads, there's a trio (or a trifecta ... or better yet, a triumvirate) of classics that you'll find everywhere you go: egg, chicken, and tuna salads. What you won't find everywhere are salads this memorable. In each one, we keep the ingredients simple, but we add a twist. The deviled egg salad has a kick from Tabasco and mustard. The tuna salad has shredded celery for crunch and sweet pickles for an unusual bite. The chicken salad is mixed with mayonnaise, then tossed with just a bit of honey for a subtle sweetness. Make them all together or one at a time for an easy Sunday afternoon lunch.

trio egg salad

Serves 4

6 large eggs

2 to 3 tablespoons mayonnaise

1 tablespoon smooth Dijon mustard

1 teaspoon Tabasco sauce

Salt and freshly ground black pepper to taste

1 head of red leaf lettuce, to serve

1. Place the eggs in a large pot of water. Bring to a boil, then remove the pot from the heat. Keep the eggs in the water for 10 minutes. Then transfer the eggs to a large bowl of cold water and allow to cool for 3 minutes.

2. Peel the eggs. Slice them into small dice or, using an egg cutter, slice lengthwise, then again widthwise.

3. Place the diced eggs in a large bowl and mix with the mayonnaise, mustard, and Tabasco. Season with salt and pepper to taste. Mix gently to combine.

4. To serve, place 2 lettuce leaves on each of 4 plates. Divide the salad evenly among them. If you are serving the egg salad as part of the Trio, scoop about 1 cup of each salad onto each lettuce-lined plate.

trio chicken salad

Serves 4

4 6- to 8-ounce chicken breasts

1 cup mayonnaise

½ teaspoon onion powder

1 tablespoon honey

Salt and freshly ground black pepper to taste

1 head of red leaf lettuce, to serve

1. Bring a large pot of water to a boil. While the water is heating, place the chicken breasts between 2 sheets of waxed paper and pound them to an even thickness.

2. Place the chicken in the boiling water and cook for 10 minutes, or until cooked through. When the chicken is done, drain and allow it to cool slightly. Using your hands, tear the chicken into bite-size pieces.

3. In a large bowl, mix the chicken with the mayonnaise and onion powder. Add the honey and season with the salt and pepper.

4. To serve, place 2 lettuce leaves on each of 4 plates. Divide the salad evenly among them. If you are serving the chicken salad as part of the Trio, scoop about 1 cup of each salad onto each lettuce-lined plate.

trio tuna salad

Serves 4

3 6-ounce cans of solid white tuna, drained

¼ cup minced sweet pickles

¼ cup shredded celery (1 stalk)

¾ cup mayonnaise, or to taste

Salt and freshly ground black pepper to taste

1 head of red leaf lettuce, to serve

1. In a large bowl, combine the tuna, pickles, and celery. Stir in the mayonnaise until evenly distributed. Season with the salt and pepper.

2. To serve, place 2 lettuce leaves on each of 4 plates. Divide the salad evenly among them. If you are serving the tuna salad as part of the Trio, scoop about 1 cup of each salad onto each lettuce-lined plate.

Mayonnaise has been around a lot longer than diners, but this necessary condiment complements so many foods that it's worth knowing about. The history of mayonnaise goes like this: in 1756, the French chef of the Duke of Richelieu was preparing a feast in honor of his employer's victory over the British at Port Mahon. But, "*Mon dieu!*," there was no cream to make his usual special sauce that called for blending cream with eggs. The chef substituted olive oil for the cream, and the resulting goodness is dubbed "Mahonnaise" to honor the big win.

Flash forward to 1905, when Richard Hellmann — a German immigrant who owned a deli in New York City — offered his customers mayonnaise homemade by his wife. The recipe was so good that people started asking to buy it. Mr. Hellmann obliged, and originally, there were two versions offered, one with a blue ribbon. The blue ribbon recipe became such a hit that Mr. Hellmann designed a label featuring the ribbon and placed the condiment in glass jars. Today, you can get one of those very labels for yourself at almost any grocery store in the country. If you live west of the Rocky Mountains, you'll see Hellmann's sold under the brand "Best Foods," but that beaming blue label is still there.

chopped health salad

Serves 4

One of life's little frustrations (and I do mean little) is eating a salad and not being able to get a bite of everything on your fork at the same time. But the wide assortment of raw and roasted vegetables in this salad is cut small, so it helps you shovel a bite of each flavor onto your fork in a nice, dainty way.

1 medium-sized eggplant

1½ tablespoons salt

1 cup small-diced yellow squash (1 medium-sized squash)

1 cup small-diced zucchini (1 medium-sized zucchini)

3 tablespoons olive oil

1 tablespoon freshly ground black pepper

1 cup cucumber, peeled, seeded, and diced (1 medium-sized cucumber)

3 tomatoes, sliced into ¼-inch rounds

2 portobello mushroom caps, diced

4 cups mixed greens

Balsamic Vinaigrette (page 126)

1. Preheat the oven to 350° F. Slice the eggplant in half and sprinkle ½ tablespoon of the salt on each of the flat sides. Allow juices to drain for 20 minutes. Rinse off any remaining salt. Then dice the eggplant into 4 cups of small cubes and place them in a baking dish with the yellow squash and zucchini.

2. Toss the cubed vegetables with the olive oil, remaining salt, and pepper. Roast them in the oven for 30 minutes, until softened, but not limp. Then allow the mixture to cool completely.

3. Meanwhile, toss the cucumber, tomatoes, and portobellos in a large bowl.

4. To serve each salad: place 1 cup of mixed greens on a plate. Top with 1 cup of roasted vegetables, then add 1 cup of the cucumber mix. Serve with Balsamic Vinaigrette.

warm taco salad

Serves 4

This is another one of our dishes inspired by foods of other cultures. If you make this on a hot summer day and spice it up a little, you'll get that sweaty thing goin' on — so when a breeze blows by, you're as cool as a freezer full of ice cream. (Or a cucumber, but I'm sure you're cooler than that.)

Serve this with beer and lots of tortilla chips. The juices from the meat will flow down into the lettuce — so you don't even need to make a dressing.

2 tablespoons vegetable oil

1½ cups chopped Spanish onion (1 large onion)

2 jalapeño peppers, minced (more or less as preferred)

2 pounds ground beef

1 tablespoon Cajun spice mix (or Goya "Hot" Adobo seasoning)

2 tablespoons ground cumin

2 garlic cloves, minced

2 cups canned plum tomatoes

1 head of iceberg lettuce, shredded

For garnish

2 cups (8 ounces) shredded Cheddar cheese

½ cup sour cream

½ cup Lively Tomato Salsa (page 121)

Corn tortilla chips, to serve

1. In a tall-sided sauté pan, heat the oil over medium heat. Sauté the onion and peppers for 3 minutes, until just soft. Add the beef and sauté, breaking up the meat with a spatula for 8 to 10 minutes, until cooked through. Drain the fat from the pan.

2. Add the Cajun spice, cumin, garlic, and tomatoes with their juices. Break up the tomatoes and any clumps of meat that have formed. Bring to a boil, then simmer for 6 to 8 minutes, until thick.

3. Divide the shredded lettuce among 4 plates. Divide the meat evenly and place on top of the lettuce.

4. Sprinkle ½ cup shredded Cheddar over each salad. On the side of each, add 2 tablespoons of sour cream and 2 tablespoons of salsa. Serve with tortilla chips.

chinese chicken salad

Listen, if you find yourself in Beijing, you're not going to find this dish. But if you're having Chinese night at home, you'll make your guests happy, for sure. This salad contrasts the sweetness of the soy dressing against the tartness of the Mandarin oranges — all with the crunch of the lo mien noodles. There's a lot going on, but it's kinda like the yin-yang symbol: evenly balanced.

4 6- to 8-ounce chicken breasts

½ cup soy sauce

¾ cup teriyaki sauce

½ cup vegetable oil

2 scallions, chopped (white and green parts)

2 tablespoons grated fresh ginger

Ground white pepper to taste

4 cups mixed greens

1 15-ounce can Mandarin oranges, drained

½ cup toasted, sliced almonds

1 cup Chinese lo mein noodles

1. Bring a pot of water to a boil. While the water is heating, place the chicken between 2 sheets of waxed paper and pound to an even thickness. Poach the breasts in the boiling water for 10 minutes, or until cooked through.

2. Meanwhile, in a large bowl, mix the soy sauce, teriyaki sauce, vegetable oil, scallions, and ginger. Whisk the dressing thoroughly to combine. Season with white pepper to taste.

3. Remove the chicken from the water and drain. Allow the chicken to cool for 5 minutes, or until cool enough to handle, then slice it into bite-sized pieces. Toss the chicken in the dressing, then allow it to marinate for 10 minutes or more, if time permits.

4. To serve each salad: Place 1 cup of mixed greens on a plate. Top with ¼ of the chicken salad. Place 6 to 8 orange slices around each salad. Then over each salad, sprinkle 2 tablespoons of almonds and ¼ cup of noodles.

southwestern shrimp salad

This salad was in the original cast of *Comfort Diner: The Musical,* but it has since retired from the stage to pursue a film career. Well, sort of. The truth is that I'm always coming up with new salads and rotating them onto the menu. This was an early one, and it was one of my favorites because it's elegant, refreshing, and really easy to make. It deserves an encore performance — at the diner and in your kitchen.

24 medium to large shrimp, peeled and deveined

2 cups fresh corn kernels (about 3 ears of corn)

½ cup lime juice (from 4 to 5 limes)

1 tablespoon honey

1 cup olive oil

Tabasco sauce to taste

Salt and freshly ground black pepper to taste

1 head of iceberg lettuce, shredded

1 cup canned black beans, drained (from 1 16-ounce can)

1 mango, peeled, pitted, and sliced

1 avocado, peeled, pitted, and sliced

1 cup sour cream

1 cup Lively Tomato Salsa (page 121)

1. Bring a large pot of water to a boil. Add the shrimp and cook for 1 to 2 minutes, until shrimp are pink and opaque. Drain and allow to cool. When cooled, slice each shrimp in half lengthwise.

2. Meanwhile, in a separate pot bring 2 cups of water to a boil. Add the corn kernels and cook for 3 minutes. Drain and set aside.

3. In a small bowl, mix the lime juice, honey, olive oil, and Tabasco. Season with salt and pepper. Whisk thoroughly to combine. Pour the dressing over the shrimp and toss lightly.

4. To assemble: Evenly divide the lettuce among 4 plates. Top with shrimp at the center. Sprinkle ½ cup of the corn and ¼ cup of the black beans over each salad. Arrange 3 or 4 slices each of mango and avocado on the outer edge of each salad. Scoop ¼ cup of sour cream and ¼ cup of salsa onto the opposite edge.

comfort diner grilled chicken salad

Serves 4

This is our signature chicken salad, and it contains so many ingredients that I love to eat. (Hey, what's the point of opening a restaurant if you can't serve dishes you yourself want to eat?) I'm a big fan of warm goat cheese and artichokes. The chickpeas are so good for you, as are the greens. This is just a delicious, satisfying salad that makes a colorful, attractive presentation — whether you make one large salad or four individual ones.

4 6- to 8-ounce chicken breasts

¼ cup olive oil

4 cups mixed greens

8 quartered fresh plum tomatoes (or 8 sun-dried tomatoes in oil)

8 artichokes, halved, marinated, or packed in water, as preferred

8 ounces plain goat cheese (2 small logs)

½ cup canned chickpeas

Balsamic Vinaigrette (page 126)

1. Place the chicken breasts between 2 sheets of waxed paper and pound to an even thickness.

2. Brush a grill pan with 2 tablespoons olive oil. (If using a sauté pan, coat the pan with 2 table-spoons of olive oil.) Bring the pan to medium high heat and cook two of the chicken breasts for 8 to 10 minutes per side, until golden brown and cooked through. Repeat with the remaining oil and chicken breasts. When the chicken is cool enough to handle, slice it into long strips. Keep warm.

3. To assemble each salad: Place 1 cup mixed greens on a plate and top with several chicken strips. Add 8 wedges of tomatoes and 4 artichoke halves. Divide the goat cheese into 4 portions and place one at the center of each salad. Sprinkle each salad with 2 tablespoons of chickpeas. Serve with Balsamic Vinaigrette.

chicken caesar salad

Serves 4

Caesar conquered Rome, and Caesar salads have conquered restaurant menus. A diner's gotta have one, and this is ours. With the chicken, this makes a satisfying lunch or a light dinner. Try our Creamy Caesar Dressing for an easy version of the classic — with extra zip.

4 6- to 8-ounce chicken breasts

¼ cup olive oil

1 head of Romaine lettuce, sliced into large pieces

1 cup (4 ounces) shredded Parmesan cheese

2 cups croutons

Creamy Caesar Salad Dressing (page 128)

1. Place the chicken breasts between 2 sheets of waxed paper or plastic wrap, and pound the chicken to an even thickness.

2. Brush a grill pan with 2 tablespoons olive oil. (If using a sauté pan, coat the pan with 2 tablespoons of olive oil.) Bring the pan to medium high heat and cook two of the chicken breasts for 8 to 10 minutes per side, until golden brown and cooked through. Repeat with the remaining oil and chicken breasts. When the chicken is cool enough to handle, slice into long strips.

3. To serve each salad, divide the lettuce evenly among 4 plates. Top with 4 strips of chicken. Sprinkle ¼ cup Parmesan cheese and ½ cup croutons over each salad. Serve with Creamy Caesar Salad Dressing.

Diner Trivia

A "Hash Slinger" is a name for a diner cook that originated in the nineteenth century when hash was a popular dish in cheap restaurants. A "Soup Jockey" is a waitress, and a "Lady Bug" is a soda fountain man. The dishwasher gets the moniker of "Bubble Dancer" and the sandwich man is the "Angel." Indeed.

The origins of the Caesar salad go back to the days of Prohibition.
Hollywood types would cruise across the border for merriment in Tijuana,
Mexico, and wind up carousing at restaurants like the one owned by Caesar
Cardini, an Italian immigrant. On one packed night — July 4, 1924 — Mr.
Cardini invented his namesake salad as a main course. Originally, whole
leaves were arranged on the plate, to be eaten with the fingers. The ingredients
in the dressing — oil, salt and pepper, garlic, lemon, eggs, Worcestershire, and
Parmesan cheese — were just kitchen staples. (If you're not a fan of anchovies
in Caesar salad, you're in good company. Mr. Cardini wasn't either; apparently, his original recipe did not contain them.) Some sources suggest the
salad was invented because the house was overcrowded and the kitchen was
running out of food; something had to be put together, and Mr. Cardini
reached for what was on hand.

Whatever the case may be, this salad is a much-lauded entry in American
cuisine. In fact, in 1953, the International Society of Epicures pronounced
the salad "the greatest recipe to originate from the Americas in fifty years."

"Pass the ketchup"

chapter 4

satisfying
sandwiches

Between the Bread

At the Comfort Diner, we love to keep up traditions, but we also pride ourselves in creating new ones. The recipes in this chapter provide a perfect example of how we manage to do both. Here you'll find items that you'd expect to see on a diner menu, like the Tuna Melt and the Classic BLT. But there are also a few twists, like the Cobb Salad Sandwich and the Retro Turkey Sandwich.

When preparing any of these recipes, remember that what makes for a truly great sandwich is often not what's inside, but what's on the outside. That's right: the bread. Sad to say, bread has been unfairly maligned in the days of low-carbohydrate diets. But there's no denying the joy of a fluffy white bread, a crunchy *ciabatta,* or even a nutty, grainy whole wheat bread.

When you find the right breads that you like to use for sandwiches, you'll forget what the dieters have to say. Bread at its best will have you dizzy at the thought of wrapping your hands around two slices that hold together a mountain of turkey or ham or grilled chicken and all the toppings.

The way to get such splendid bread is to always, always, buy a loaf that is as fresh as can be. Even when it comes to a tuna melt on an English muffin, make sure you're starting with the best you can get, then turn to these recipes for the best sandwiches ever.

tuna melt

Serves 4

"You gotta have a tuna melt on the menu!" That's what my old friend Joe Fox told me when I was thinking about opening a diner. And all these years later, this classic open-face sandwich is still a staple of the Comfort Diner. We melt American cheese over the top, but it could be Cheddar or Swiss. Feel free to make it the way you like it.

4 English muffins

1 recipe Trio Tuna Salad (page 45)

8 slices tomato

8 slices American cheese

1. Preheat the oven to 250° F. Slice the English muffins in half and place them, flat side down, on a baking sheet.

2. Distribute the tuna salad evenly among the English muffins. Top each with a slice of tomato and a slice of cheese.

3. Bake in the oven for 10 to 12 minutes, until the cheese has melted and the tuna is warm all the way through.

Diner Trivia

"86"

This number now means that the kitchen has run out of an item. But the origins are debatable. One theory is that it means "Do not sell to that customer," which would make him a subject of Article 86 of the New York State Liquor Code; that explains when a customer should be cut off from anymore drinks. But there's also the bread line explanation. In the Depression, soup kitchens would cook enough for eighty-five people. If you were the eighty-sixth, you went hungry.

A tuna melt can be made using any bread, but die-hard diner folk know that the authentic version *must* be made with an English muffin. And the history of those muffins shows us another fine example of how American food culture was shaped by the ingenuity of its immigrants.

Samuel B. Thomas, a Plymouth, England, native, came to New York City and promptly opened a bakery on Ninth Avenue. Around 1880, he became known for his crumpetlike muffins made on a grill instead of in the oven. The bakery delivered the muffins to hotels and restaurants all over town. The business was handed over to his family in 1919. Today, the brand is owned by George Weston Bakeries.

How these unusual muffins came to be the primary vehicle for tuna and melted cheese is a mystery. But here's my guess. The round shape is perfect for holding a scoop of tuna, and if the tuna is a bit liquidy, the firm English muffin will soak up the liquid without falling apart.

reuben sandwich

Serves 4

Whenever I make a Reuben I get a college flashback. I was working at a really busy sandwich counter. One day, this customer comes up during the main lunch rush. Instead of saying "Hi" or anything, he shouts at me: "*Reuben!*" And I said, "No. *Ira!*" Boy, did that steam him. (But I got a chuckle.)

If you live in a place where you can buy great corned beef, by all means, do it. But if not, I suggest making this with turkey. The Reuben is pretty versatile, so try regular or smoked turkey, but don't bother with meat that's not top quality.

¼ cup (½ stick) unsalted butter, softened

8 slices rye bread

½ cup Thousand Island dressing

16 thick slices corned beef or turkey

8 slices Swiss cheese

1 cup sauerkraut

1. To assemble each sandwich: Spread ½ teaspoon of the butter on one side of each bread slice. Place the bread, butter side down, on a clean flat surface.

2. Spread 2 tablespoons of the dressing on the inside of 1 slice. Top with 4 slices of corned beef or turkey, then 2 slices of Swiss cheese. Add 3 to 4 tablespoons of sauerkraut. Close the sandwich with another slice of bread.

3. In a sauté pan at medium heat or a griddle at 250°F, melt 1 tablespoon of the butter. Heat the sandwich for 2 minutes on each side.

4. Flip the sandwich again and heat for 1 minute more on each side. Both sides of the bread should be lightly toasted and the cheese melted. Repeat with remaining sandwiches, adding more butter as needed.

There is a sizzling-hot debate over the origins of the Reuben sandwich.
And it's kind of an East Coast versus Midwest thing. One story goes that
Arnold Reuben, owner of Reuben's Restaurant in New York City, created the
grilled sandwich in 1914 for Annette Seelos, an actress who worked with
Charlie Chaplin.

A competing story asserts that a wholesale grocer named Reuben
Kolalofsky put together the now-classic bite at the Blackstone Hotel in
Omaha in the early 1920s. The invention is said to have been created during
a late-night poker game at the hotel, and the establishment's owner dubbed
the sandwich with the grocer's name. In 1956, a waitress at the hotel sent
the recipe to a national sandwich contest — and it won first prize.

Either way, the original combination consisted of corned beef, Swiss
cheese, and sauerkraut served on rye bread. And it's a safe bet that this sandwich can please both actresses and poker pals — and everyone in between.

cobb salad sandwich

Serves 4

When I was first developing recipes for the restaurant, I made this sandwich all the time for my wife, Sandy. It's been on the menu since we opened, and it's still going strong. My guess is that people like it because there are so many tastes at the same time: tangy blue cheese, crispy bacon, smooth avocado, meaty chicken. And you get almost all of it in each delicious bite.

4 6- to 8-ounce chicken breasts

¼ cup olive oil

12 slices bacon

8 slices country-style bread

½ cup Blue Cheese Dressing (page 129)

2 avocados, peeled, pitted, and sliced in eighths

8 leaves of Romaine lettuce

4 slices tomato

1. Place the chicken between 2 sheets of waxed paper and pound to an even thickness.

2. Brush a grill pan with 2 tablespoons olive oil. (If using a sauté pan, coat the pan with 2 tablespoons of olive oil.) Bring the pan to medium high heat and cook two of the chicken breasts for 8 to 10 minutes per side, until golden brown and cooked through. Repeat with the remaining oil and chicken breasts.

3. Meanwhile, cook the bacon until crispy using your preferred method. Place the bacon on paper towels to remove excess fat.

4. To assemble one sandwich: Place 2 slices of bread on a clean, flat surface. Spread 2 tablespoons of Blue Cheese dressing on 1 bread slice. On the other slice, place 1 chicken breast and 3 slices of bacon. Top with 4 avocado slices, 2 leaves of lettuce, and 1 tomato slice. Close the sandwich with the slice of bread covered with the dressing. Slice in half and serve. Repeat to make the remaining sandwiches.

Every now and then a customer will ask for the Cobb Salad

Sandwich as a salad. That's only fitting — Cobb Salad has a long-standing place in American food culture. It was originally created in 1926 at the famous Brown Derby restaurant in Los Angeles owned by Bob Cobb. The story goes that Mr. Cobb wanted to use up some leftover ingredients, so he made himself a salad from all the bits and pieces. The salad made its way from the kitchen to the dining rooms and became a Hollywood staple. The traditional ingredients are lettuce, chopped chicken, bacon, hard-boiled eggs, tomato, avocado, scallions, watercress, and blue cheese — with a vinaigrette dressing.

There are variations, of course. Cheddar cheese can be substituted for the blue cheese — in which case a creamy blue cheese dressing (like ours on page 129) can be used instead of vinaigrette. Chopped fresh turkey can replace the chicken. But without all the other items listed above, a Cobb Salad just isn't a proper Cobb Salad.

retro turkey sandwich

Serves 4

Remember this one from the '80s? Seems like it went out of style, but it still tastes good. It's got all kinds of healthful ingredients and a low-fat dressing, plus whole-grain bread. If you start quoting lines from *Back to the Future,* I'll understand. This sandwich is good enough to make you wish you had a Flux Capacitor.

8 slices whole-grain bread

Honey Mustard Dressing
   (page 120)

12 thick slices roasted turkey
   (or 16 deli-style slices)

8 slices Muenster cheese

1 cup alfalfa sprouts

1 cup shredded carrots
   (2 medium-sized carrots)

2 avocados, peeled, pitted,
   and sliced in eighths

8 slices tomato

1. To assemble each sandwich: Place 2 slices of bread on a clean, flat surface. Swipe 1 slice of bread with 2 tablespoons of Honey Mustard Dressing.

2. On the other slice of bread, place 3 slices of turkey, followed by 2 slices of Muenster and $\frac{1}{4}$ cup of alfalfa sprouts. Add $\frac{1}{4}$ cup of carrots, 4 avocado slices, and 2 tomato slices.

3. Top with the remaining slice of bread, honey mustard down. Repeat with remaining sandwiches.

Diner Trivia

When you're sitting in a diner booth, you're actually in the "gallery." And if you've got four people in your party, you're a "Bridge," which comes from the card game. Three of anything in a diner is called a crowd, because, you know, three's a crowd. (Or is it company? You decide!)

classic blt

What makes our version of this classic diner sandwich special is that we use whole-grain bread (instead of white) and red leaf lettuce (instead of iceberg). Whole-grain bread has more texture — plus it's better for you. And red leaf lettuce is softer than iceberg, making for a delicate contrast with the bacon. With all the bacon on this sandwich, you'll get plenty of crispy, crunchy sensations. And if you want a lighter version, substitute turkey bacon.

20 slices bacon

8 slices whole-grain bread

½ cup mayonnaise

1 head of red leaf lettuce

8 slices tomatoes

1. Cook the bacon until crispy using your preferred method. Place on paper towels to remove excess fat.

2. To assemble one sandwich: Swipe the inside of 1 slice of bread with mayonnaise. Place 2 lettuce leaves on the bread, followed by 5 slices of bacon and 2 slices of tomato. Top with the remaining slice of bread. Slice in half and serve. Repeat to make the remaining sandwiches.

Diner Night at Home

Let a rainy day turn into a cheerful evening by declaring your very own Diner Night. You can play the short-order cook by firing up a griddle and letting your crew put in their orders for one of two classic diner sandwiches. Don't forget to turn on some '50s music and be sure to have a good time, baby.

Grandma's Chicken Soup (page 35)

Classic BLT (above) or Classic Grilled Cheese sandwiches (page 71)

Not-Fried Fries (page 116)

Mile-High Apple Pie (page 148)

grilled chicken club

Serves 4

Chicken club sandwiches usually come sliced into four triangles — and as soon as you pick one up, you've got to hold on for dear life before the chicken falls out or the tomato slips away. Well, that sort of explosion won't happen with this chicken club. We slice it right down the middle, no four ways about it. So go ahead and enjoy this tasty combination. It's not going anywhere you don't want it to.

16 slices bacon

4 6- to 8-ounce chicken breasts

12 slices white bread

1 head of red leaf lettuce

8 tomato slices

½ cup mayonnaise

1. Cook the bacon until crispy using your preferred method. Place on paper towels to remove the excess fat.

2. Meanwhile, grill or sauté the chicken for 8 to 10 minutes per side, until cooked through.

3. To assemble one sandwich: On a slice of bread, place 1 chicken breast, then 4 slices of bacon. Top with another slice of bread. Place 2 tomato slices and 2 leaves of lettuce on the bread. Swipe another slice of bread with mayonnaise and close the sandwich. Cut the sandwich in half to serve. Repeat to make the remaining sandwiches.

Diner Trivia

The early diners were simple horse-drawn lunch wagons. In 1872 Walter Scott brought the wagon filled with sandwiches and light fare to factory workers in Providence, Rhode Island. Over the years, competition grew and one wagon owner finally realized that in a larger space, people could sit down to eat, rather than stand outside. Old trolley cars were rolled to a convenient spot and converted to diners. Gradually, manufacturers began to create "lunch cars" that had a modified shape of a rail car. Diners became modular, prefabricated structures set down wherever the owner wanted. And as the menus expanded from factory-worker lunches to all meals for all folks, the term diners—as in a railroad's diner car—gained currency.

sliced steak sandwich with mushrooms on garlic toast

Serves 4

This sandwich was our precursor to the cheesesteak, and it's a snap to make at home. When you bite into this combination of cheese, meat, and mushrooms with just a hint of garlic, you get a true taste of comfort food.

4 hero rolls

1 garlic clove

8 slices mozzarella cheese

2 tablespoons vegetable oil

3 cups white mushrooms, thinly sliced (about 12 mushrooms)

2 pounds thin-sliced beef cutlets, or a whole strip steak

1. Preheat the oven to 200°F. Slice the rolls through the middle, but do not slice all the way through. Place the rolls opened up in the oven for 5 minutes, until just crisp. Remove from the oven. Rub a clove of garlic over the inside of the rolls.

2. In a sauté pan, warm the oil over medium heat. Add the mushrooms and sauté for 3 to 4 minutes, until soft and dark brown. Place the mushrooms in a bowl and set aside.

3. If using sliced beef, place it in the pan and sear quickly, for 1 to 2 minutes on each side, until browned. If using a whole steak, sear on both sides until done to your preference. Transfer the steak to a cutting board and slice into strips.

4. Place 2 slices of cheese on the inside of each roll and return to the oven for 2 minutes until the cheese is melted. Remove the rolls from the oven and divide the meat evenly among the sandwiches. Top with the cooked mushrooms. Serve warm.

crab burger

You can serve these crab cakes as we do at the Comfort Diner — on a bun, with our Tangy Remoulade Sauce on the side — or you can serve them straight, as a light lunch with a salad or as the main course for dinner. Either way, they're a crowd-pleaser. As you'll see from the recipe, we don't load our crab cakes with pounds of bread crumbs or other filler. What you get is a full crab flavor enhanced by fresh herbs and a little spicy kick.

1 tablespoon lemon juice

3 tablespoons chopped fresh chives

2 tablespoons minced red bell pepper

1 tablespoon dry mustard

¼ teaspoon cayenne pepper

20 ounces fresh lump crabmeat

½ cup mayonnaise

3 dashes of Tabasco sauce, or to taste

2 cups plain bread crumbs, for coating

4 soft round sandwich rolls

1 head of red leaf lettuce

8 slices tomato

Tangy Remoulade Sauce (page 124), to serve

1. Preheat the oven to 325°F. In a large bowl, mix the lemon juice, chives, bell pepper, dry mustard, and cayenne pepper. Add the crabmeat, mayonnaise, and Tabasco. Mix until evenly combined.

2. Form into 4 evenly sized balls, then flatten into 4 patties. Spread the bread crumbs on a plate and coat the patties with them.

3. Place the patties on a greased cookie sheet or one lined with parchment paper. Bake in the oven for about 20 minutes, until the patties are set and firm.

4. Place each crab cake in a soft roll and top with 2 lettuce leaves and 2 tomato slices. Serve with Tangy Remoulade Sauce.

imagination burger

Serves 4

Ever go to a diner and see thirty-six different burgers on the menu? Then once you look closer, it's just six ingredients changed around. There's the Swiss Burger, the Swiss Mushroom Burger, the Cheddar Mushroom Burger, and so on.

It's hooey, I tell ya. At the Comfort Diner, I let people use their imaginations. The menu lists all the ingredients, and folks can build their own burger. I love it when customers order one with everything. That's four different cheeses, avocado, bacon, onion, and more. It starts out as an eight-ounce burger, so once you load it up with everything, you could be eating two pounds of food. And what's more fun than that? Well, use your imagination.

1 pound lean ground beef

1 teaspoon salt

1 teaspoon freshly ground black pepper

4 kaiser rolls, sliced

1 head of red leaf lettuce (optional)

8 tomato slices (optional)

1 red onion, sliced (optional)

And your choice of

Cheddar cheese

American cheese

Muenster cheese

Mozzarella

Blue Cheese Dressing (page 129)

Crispy bacon

Avocado

Three-Bean Vegetarian Chili (page 90)

Sautéed onions

Sautéed mushrooms

(And anything else you like)

1. In a large bowl, mix by hand the ground beef, salt, and pepper. Divide the meat evenly into 4 patties.

2. On a grill or a sauté pan (with the exhaust fan running) on medium-high heat (or on an outdoor grill), cook the beef patties for 5 minutes per side for medium rare, 6 minutes per side for medium. If you are adding cheese, place the cheese on the burger for 1 minute while it is still cooking.

3. Place cooked burgers inside the sliced kaiser rolls. Top with lettuce, tomato, and red onion, and whatever else suits you and your family's fancy.

"Cheese, please"

chapter 5

grilled cheese galore

The Ultimate Meltdown

Crispy on the outside, smooth and gooey on the inside, the classic grilled cheese sandwich is comfort food at its best. When grilled just right, the thin slices of white bread are evenly toasted to a golden shade of brown. And the tangy American cheese softens into a layer of orange goodness. It takes you back to the days when your feet dangled from the counter stool and holding hands was a requirement for crossing the street.

These sandwiches are still a bona fide winner with children, but I see it time and time again: parents will reach over to "help" the little ones finish. Well, listen up Daddy-o: get your own!

With these recipes, that's easy to do. We've gone way beyond American cheese—here are eleven different ways to serve up melted cheese on bread. The cheeses range from Swiss to Boursin to goat cheese. The breads range from rye to raisin to rosemary. But there's one consistent ingredient through it all: butter. Nothing helps along a perfect pairing of cheese and bread like a generous swipe of butter; it's what gives the bread that good greasy crunch. When you're making these at home, don't be shy about the butter. The sandwiches need it. And if you're needing some happy food, then so do you.

Grilled cheese is a signature sandwich at the Comfort Diner. We love it so much that during the month of February, we make a different kind of grilled cheese every day. It's called our Grilled Cheese Meltdown, and we go a little nutty for this gooey treat.

This chapter contains eleven of my variations on the classic, and in every case, the secret to a perfect sandwich lies in two little words: *low* and *slow*. Always keep the heat low and cook the sandwich slowly. All together now: slo-o-o-wly. This will keep the bread from burning and allow the cheese to melt evenly. There's nothing worse than putting a sandwich onto high heat, then winding up with burnt bread and cold cheese in the middle.

Another key step is to spread the butter evenly on the slice of bread. But if you forget (or don't have time) to soften the butter, just throw some butter in the pan, swirl it around, and place the bread on it. Give the bread a little time to soak up the butter, and it will still be distributed evenly.

classic grilled cheese

Serves 4

The best place to start is with the original: the grilled American cheese sandwich. We use four—count 'em, four—slices of cheese, which is a little cheesier than average. But that's what makes this a sandwich that both kids and grown-ups can't do without.

About ¼ cup (½ stick) unsalted butter, softened

8 slices white bread

16 slices American cheese

1. To assemble each sandwich: Spread ½ teaspoon butter on 1 side of each bread slice. Place bread, butter side down, on a clean, flat surface.

2. Place 4 slices of cheese on 1 slice of bread. Close the sandwich by placing the remaining slice of bread on the cheese, butter side out.

3. Melt 1 tablespoon butter in a sauté pan on medium-low heat or a griddle at 250° F. Place the sandwich on the heat for 2 minutes.

4. Using a spatula, flip the sandwich and cook for 2 minutes more. Both sides of the bread should be lightly toasted. Repeat with the remaining sandwiches, adding butter to the pan as needed.

There are certain foods that go so well together that the pairings have become part of American popular culture. And that's certainly true of grilled cheese and tomato soup. If you need a soup to serve your grilled cheese alongside, look no further than page 36, where you'll find the Comfort Diner's Chilled Tomato Soup. It's a chunky cold soup loaded with roasted tomatoes.

But if you're a purist, you might want to head to the grocery store for a can of Campbell's Tomato Soup. It was the first variety in Campbell's lineup of condensed soups, introduced in 1897 by the Camden, New Jersey-based company. Since that time, the sweet flavor of the soup, which is balanced by the natural acidity of the tomatoes, has been the perfect complement to grilled, buttery bread and melted, creamy cheese.

Not to be outdone, Progresso came up with a soup recipe that combines the two foods in the same serving. For a Grilled Cheese—Tomato Soup, just heat up some tomato soup and toss in croutons and shredded Colby cheese, which should melt on contact. It's not quite grilled, but it's a clever notion just the same!

grilled triple cheese

Serves 4

If one cheese is good, then, hey, "three's company." You can play around with the lineup of cheese, if you like. Try mixing in slices of American or pepper jack for kicks. But please, keep the bad TV jokes and slapstick to a minimum.

About ¼ cup (½ stick) unsalted butter, softened	8 slices white bread 8 slices Cheddar cheese	8 slices mozzarella cheese 8 slices Swiss cheese

1. To assemble each sandwich: Spread ½ teaspoon butter on 1 side of each bread slice. Place the bread, butter side down, on a clean, flat surface.

2. Place 2 slices of Cheddar, 2 slices of mozzarella, and 2 slices of Swiss on 1 slice of bread. Close the sandwich by placing the remaining slice of bread on the cheese, butter side out.

3. Melt 1 tablespoon of butter in a sauté pan on medium heat or a griddle at 250°F. Place the sandwich on the heat for 2 minutes.

4. Using a spatula, flip the sandwich and heat for 2 minutes more. Flip again for about 1 minute on each side to be sure that all the cheese is melted. Both sides of the bread should be lightly toasted. Repeat with the remaining sandwiches, adding butter to the pan as needed.

black bean quesadilla

Serves 4

During Comfort Diner's Grilled Cheese Meltdown, we go global by serving up grilled cheese sandwiches from lots of different cultures. This one's for our Mexican delegation. And if you wind up with some extra tortillas, you can mix up a treat the next morning. Try making a breakfast quesadilla by adding two scrambled eggs and cooked bacon to this recipe.

4 12-inch flour tortillas

1 cup (4 ounces) shredded pepper jack cheese

1 cup (4 ounces) shredded Cheddar cheese

1 cup canned black beans, drained (from 1 16-ounce can)

2 avocados, peeled, pitted, and sliced in eighths

$\frac{1}{4}$ cup vegetable oil

1. To assemble each quesadilla: Place 1 tortilla on a flat work surface. Slice the tortilla down the middle. Sprinkle half of the tortilla with $\frac{1}{4}$ cup of pepper jack, $\frac{1}{4}$ cup of Cheddar, $\frac{1}{4}$ cup of black beans, and 4 slices of avocado. Top with the other half of the tortilla.

2. In a large sauté pan on medium heat or a griddle at 250° F, heat 1 tablespoon of the oil.

3. Place the quesadilla on the hot surface. Heat for 2 minutes on each side, until the tortilla is crispy and the cheese is melted. Repeat with the remaining quesadillas and oil.

Diner Trivia

Though diners were initially set up close to factories, offices, and anywhere people were gathering in town, they also started cropping up on the highways. In the late 1920s, the roadside diner began to take hold as a way of serving car travelers. As highways improved and expanded, someone had to feed all those happy drivers. Stopping at a diner would quickly become a necessary part of the ultimate American experience: the road trip.

The way we make quesadillas at the diner is pretty standard, but at home, you've got the opportunity to toss in whatever happens to be on hand. Here are a few suggestions for substitutions or additional ingredients that will add some spark in between your tortillas. For a quesadilla party, you can offer several options and allow guests to make their own. In that case, you might want to offer smaller-sized tortillas so that everyone gets to try a few different options. As always, get creative! And send us a postcard when you come up with one that's a hit.

Sautéed mushrooms and spinach

Roasted poblano chiles (peeled and seeded)

Green chiles

Roasted zucchini and sweet peppers

Fresh corn and basil

Crabmeat

Shrimp

Roasted pork, beef, or chicken

Sautéed chorizo sausage

Sautéed ground beef

Scrambled eggs

Manchego cheese

Pinto beans

sweet georgia brown

Serves 4

The Harlem Globetrotters' theme song, "Sweet Georgia Brown," was my inspiration for this sandwich. A few years ago, the team was in town the same week that I was to be interviewed by a local television station. The producers wanted to do a little cross-promotion, so they asked if they could send the Globetrotters to the Comfort Diner. I thought about how to make a sandwich in their honor and decided to use the theme song. I ended up with a "sweet" sandwich by using peach preserves and ricotta. Those peaches stand for "Georgia." And the cinnamon toast is "brown." And hence, the Sweet Georgia Brown grilled cheese. How's that for spur-of-the-moment sandwich making?

About ¼ cup (½ stick) unsalted butter, softened

8 slices raisin bread

½ cup peach preserves

1 cup ricotta cheese

1. To assemble each sandwich: Spread ½ teaspoon butter on 1 side of each slice. Place butter side down on a clean, flat surface.

2. Spread the peach preserves on the inside of each slice. Scoop ¼ cup ricotta onto the inside of 1 slice. Close the sandwich by placing the remaining slice of bread on the cheese, butter side out.

3. Melt 1 tablespoon butter in a large sauté pan on medium heat or a griddle at 250°F. Place the sandwich onto the heat for 1 minute.

4. Using a spatula, flip the sandwich. Heat for 1 minute more. (This sandwich needs less time to cook than others because the cheese is soft.) Both sides of the bread should be lightly toasted. Repeat with the remaining sandwiches, adding butter to the pan as needed.

mediterranean melt

From time to time I've been invited on morning television shows to demonstrate some of the recipes from the Comfort Diner. I've made a dozen or so grilled cheeses during my visits to the *Today Show*. But this one was the biggest hit with Al Roker, who swooned: "I can taste the Aegean Sea!"

My advice is to take the time to oven-roast the tomatoes. Sure, you can use sun-dried tomatoes and it will still be delicious. But if you have the time, the addition of these sweet, soft tomatoes cooked right in your own oven really makes this sandwich.

4 plum tomatoes, quartered (or 8 sun-dried tomatoes)

About ¼ cup (½ stick) unsalted butter, softened

8 slices rosemary bread (or country white)

½ cup pesto

8 ounces plain goat cheese (2 small logs)

1. Preheat the oven to 350°F. Place the quartered tomatoes, flat side down, in a large baking dish and roast for 30 minutes. Remove from the oven and allow to cool.

2. To assemble each melt: Spread ½ teaspoon butter on 1 side of each bread slice. Place bread, butter side down, on a clean, flat surface. Spread 2 tablespoons of pesto on the inside of 1 slice. Place 4 tomato slices on top of the pesto.

3. On the other bread slice, evenly spread 2 ounces of goat cheese. Close the sandwich by placing the slice of bread with the cheese on top of the tomatoes, butter side out.

4. Melt 1 tablespoon butter in a large sauté pan on medium heat or a griddle at 250°F. Place the sandwich on the heat for 1 minute.

5. Using a spatula, flip the sandwich and heat for 1 minute on the other side, until the goat cheese has melted. Both sides of the bread should be lightly toasted. Repeat with the remaining sandwiches, adding butter to the pan as needed.

turkey, cheddar, *and* cranberry melt

Serves 4

Why combine turkey, Cheddar, and cranberry sauce on a sandwich? Hmm, let's see. Because it tastes great together! It's salty, sweet, and tart all at the same time — a perfect combination of Thanksgiving flavors without all the work.

About ¼ cup (½ stick) unsalted butter, softened

8 slices white bread

½ cup fresh Cranberry Sauce (page 125)

8 slices Cheddar cheese

8 thick slices turkey (or 16 thin deli slices)

1. To assemble each sandwich: Spread ½ teaspoon butter on 1 side of each bread slice. Place bread, butter side down, on a clean, flat surface.

2. Swipe 1 side of 1 slice with 2 tablespoons of the cranberry sauce. Top with 2 slices of cheese and 2 slices of turkey. Close the sandwich with the remaining slice of bread, butter side out.

3. Melt 1 tablespoon butter in a sauté pan on medium heat or a griddle at 250°F. Place the sandwich on the heat for 2 minutes.

4. Using a spatula, flip the sandwich and heat for 2 minutes more. Both sides of the bread should be lightly toasted. Repeat with the remaining sandwiches, adding butter to the pan as needed.

toasted muenster *and* ham on marble rye

Serves 4

Muenster has always been a favorite cheese of mine. Here, it's combined with ham and rye to create a tangier, toastier take on the classic ham and Swiss sandwich.

About ¼ cup (½ stick) unsalted butter, softened

8 slices marble rye bread

8 slices Muenster cheese

8 thick slices ham (or 16 thin deli slices)

1. To assemble each sandwich: Spread ½ teaspoon butter on 1 side of each bread slice. Place bread, butter side down, on a clean, flat surface.

2. Place 2 slices of cheese and 2 slices of ham on 1 slice of bread. Close the sandwich with the remaining slice of bread, butter side out.

3. Melt 1 tablespoon butter in a sauté pan on medium heat or a griddle at 250°F. Place the sandwich on the heat for 2 minutes.

4. Using a spatula, flip the sandwich and heat for 2 minutes. Both sides of the bread should be lightly toasted. Repeat with the remaining ingredients, adding butter to the pan as needed.

Diner Trivia

What's the smaller version of the diner?
The dinette.
These one-man operations were similar to the lunch wagons of yore. Customers could sidle up to the counter and get all the wholesome, good food they could at a diner. But instead of taking up as much space as a long railcar, dinettes were built about a third of the size of a regular diner.

Ever wonder where rye bread comes from? Well, here's the skinny: rye is a hardy annual cereal grass, and its seeds are used to make rye flour. This flour is darker in color than other flours (such as all-purpose), which accounts for the slightly brown color of rye bread. Pumpernickel bread is made from even darker, coarse-ground rye flour, with the addition of molasses. When rye and pumpernickel are joined together in one loaf, you wind up with a "marble rye," which you might remember from a certain episode of the popular television show *Seinfeld*. When caraway seeds are added to a light rye dough, the result is a pungent bread that's known as New York Rye.

When making the Toasted Muenster and Ham on Marble Rye (or any other) sandwich, the choice of bread is yours. Some people enjoy a mild rye taste without the pesky seeds. Others love biting into those caraway seeds that burst with flavor. As the saying goes: different strokes for different folks.

grilled cubano

Serves 4

This Cuban sandwich is another example of our international flair during our Grilled Cheese Meltdown. Though this grilled delight shares some elements with other sandwiches, the sliced pickles tucked into this meal-on-a-roll make for a perky taste surprise.

4 hero rolls

4 tablespoons yellow or deli mustard

8 slices Swiss cheese

8 thick slices turkey (or 12 thin deli slices)

8 thick slices ham (or 12 thin deli slices)

4 pickles, each cut lengthwise into 4 flat slices

¼ cup (½ stick) unsalted butter

1. To assemble each sandwich: Slice a roll in the middle without severing it in half. Brush 1 tablespoon mustard on the top half. Place 2 slices of Swiss, 2 slices of turkey, and 2 slices of ham on the bottom half. Top with pickles and close the sandwich.

2. Heat 1 tablespoon of the butter in a skillet on medium heat or on a griddle at 250°F.

3. Place the sandwich on the heat for 4 to 5 minutes on each side, until the cheese is melted and the meats are heated. To keep the sandwich together, place a sheet of aluminum foil on it and press a heavy object (such as a filled tea kettle) on top while the sandwich is cooking. Repeat with the remaining sandwiches, adding more butter to the pan as needed.

croque monsieur

There's more than one way to make a *croque monsieur*. This version was a staple of the menu at a restaurant where I worked during college. It became a favorite sandwich of mine, because it's just heaven for a cheese lover. There's cheese inside and cheese on the top, too. And how can you argue with that?

About ¼ cup (½ stick) unsalted butter, softened

8 slices white bread

4 tablespoons Thousand Island dressing

16 slices Swiss cheese

8 thick slices ham (or 16 thin deli slices)

1. Heat the broiler. To assemble each sandwich: Spread ½ teaspoon butter on 1 side of each bread slice. Place the bread, butter side down, on a clean, flat surface.

2. On 1 slice of bread, spread 1 tablespoon of Thousand Island dressing, followed by 2 slices of Swiss. Top with 2 slices of ham. Close the sandwich by placing the remaining slice of bread on the ham, butter side out.

3. Melt 1 tablespoon of the butter in a sauté pan on medium-low heat or a griddle at 225° F. Place the sandwich in the pan and heat for 2 minutes. Using a spatula, flip the sandwich and heat for 1 minute more. Both sides of the bread should be lightly toasted.

4. Place 2 slices of Swiss on top of the sandwich. Transfer the sandwich to a baking sheet and heat under the broiler for 2 minutes, or until the cheese melts. Repeat with the remaining sandwiches, adding more butter to the pan as needed.

A "croque monsieur" is a traditional French sandwich that regularly appears on the menus of bistros, which are more or less the French version of American diners. These sandwiches are typically made of ham and cheese (Swiss or Emmentaler) between two slices of white bread. The sandwich is dipped lightly in egg batter and grilled, then served with a Mornay or béchamel sauce. The name of this heavenly delight comes from the French verb *croquer*, which means to "crunch" or "crack." The *croque madame* is the same sandwich served with an egg on top.

Here in the United States, the *croque monsieur* is thought to be the grandfather of the Monte Cristo, a similar sandwich that started showing up on the West Coast in the late '40s and early '50s. The Monte Christo is served often with jam or jelly on the side, but as with many foods, the origins are a matter of lively debate.

grilled havarti *and* roasted garlic

This sandwich is so good it makes my eyes roll back in my head. The Havarti is tart and creamy. The *ciabatta* has a great texture. And roasted garlic takes on that nutty, unbelievably delicious flavor. If you've got a business meeting, you might want to spread only one side with garlic. But if you're just hanging out at home, get that garlic on both sides and go for it.

1 head garlic

1 loaf *ciabatta*, soft baguette, or Italian bread

About ¼ cup (½ stick) unsalted butter, softened

8 thin slices Havarti

1. Heat the oven to 350°F. Slice off the papery tuft from the top of the garlic head. Place the head of garlic on a baking sheet in the oven. Roast for 30 to 45 minutes, until each clove is soft.

2. To assemble each sandwich: Slice a 3-inch-long piece of bread from the loaf and cut it through the middle. Spread ½ teaspoon butter on the outside of each side of the bread. Place bread, butter side down, on a clean, flat surface.

3. Spread 1 (or 2, as preferred) garlic cloves on the inside of 1 slice. Place 2 slices of cheese on top of the garlic. Close the sandwich by placing the remaining slice of bread on the cheese, butter side out.

4. Melt 1 tablespoon butter in a sauté pan on medium-low heat or a griddle at 225°F. Place the sandwich on the heat for 2 minutes.

5. Using a spatula, flip the sandwich and keep on the heat for 2 minutes more. Both sides of the bread should be lightly toasted. Repeat with remaining sandwiches, adding butter to the pan as needed.

boursin *and* bacon on black-pepper bread

Serves 4

If you can't get your hands on black-pepper bread, never fear: a handy trick is here. Just butter some white bread, then grind some coarse black pepper onto a work surface. Press the buttered side into the pepper, and voilà! You'll get that zippy, peppery taste—which combines so well with this soft, garlicky cheese. But be careful on this one. The cheese is soft and can cook very quickly. In this case, it's okay to turn up the heat so that the bread toasts as fast as the cheese melts.

12 slices bacon

About ¼ cup (½ stick) unsalted butter, softened

1 5-ounce round Boursin cheese, quartered

8 slices black-pepper bread (see note above)

1. Cook the bacon until crispy according to your preferred method. Remove it from the heat and place on a paper towel–lined plate.

2. To assemble each sandwich: Spread ½ teaspoon of butter on 1 side of each bread slice. Place bread, butter side down, on a clean, flat surface. (If you're turning regular bread into black-pepper bread, you won't need extra butter.)

3. Spread a quarter of the cheese on 1 slice of bread. Top with 3 slices of bacon. Close the sandwich by placing the remaining slice of bread on the cheese, butter side out.

4. Melt 1 tablespoon butter in a sauté pan on medium-low heat or a griddle at 250° F. Place the sandwich on the heat for 1 minute.

5. Using a spatula, flip the sandwich and keep on the heat for 1 minute more. Both sides of the bread should be lightly toasted and the cheese just melted. Repeat with the remaining sandwiches, adding butter to the pan as needed.

"What's your special?"

chapter 6

big plates

Hearty Wholesome Meals Start Here

From Macaroni and Cheese to Mom's Meatloaf, from Comforting Chicken Potpie to Yankee Pot Roast, the Big Plates are the heart and soul of a diner. When you're at the Comfort Diner, we want you to slide into a booth, sip some fresh coffee, and order yourself a wholesome, satisfying meal. When you're at home, we hope your friends and family will crowd around your dining room table, share a laugh, and enjoy the same nourishing meals—made with that dash of TLC that's only to be found in your home kitchen.

And if you're wondering why we call them Big Plates—not "entrees," not "main courses"—there's a reason. We want our guests to feel free to mix and match as they like. There's no fixed number of courses that you should have or any particular order in which you should eat them. The only thing you should do is eat until you're good and stuffed. And that's the spirit we hope you'll catch at home with this book. This food is meant to be enjoyed, not fretted over. It's meant to be "ooohed" and "ahhed" at, but not to be awed at. So roll up those sleeves and dig right in.

macaroni *and* cheese

We make our mac and cheese with three cheeses: American, Cheddar, and fontina. The first two provide that rich smoothness that you expect from the diner standby. Then the fontina adds a subtle kick that marries well with the mustard's tang. This dish is by far the most popular item on our children's menu. Make it anytime you — or your kids — feel like a bowl of true comfort food.

¼ cup (½ stick) plus 1 tablespoon unsalted butter, plus 1 pat for greasing the baking dish

1 pound elbow macaroni

2 tablespoons olive or vegetable oil

3¼ cups whole milk

¼ cup all-purpose flour

4 slices American cheese

1 cup (4 ounces) shredded fontina cheese

1 ¼ cup shredded Cheddar cheese (5 ounces)

2½ teaspoons Dijon mustard

½ cup plain bread crumbs

1. Preheat the oven to 375° F. Butter a 9×12-inch baking dish. Bring a large pot of salted water to a boil. Cook the macaroni until al dente according to package directions. Drain and rinse with cool water. Place macaroni in a large mixing bowl and drizzle with the oil.

2. In a small saucepan, gently warm the milk. In a larger saucepan, melt the ¼ cup butter over medium-low heat. Sprinkle the flour over the butter. Whisk constantly for 2 to 3 minutes, until the flour is absorbed and the mixture is gently bubbling and lightly golden. Gradually add the milk while whisking continuously. Bring to a simmer for 3 to 4 minutes, until smooth and thickened. Stir frequently.

3. Add the American, fontina, and 1 cup of the Cheddar cheese to the mixture. Remove from the heat and stir until the cheese melts. Stir in the mustard. Pour the sauce over the macaroni and mix to combine. Transfer the macaroni to the baking dish.

4. To make the topping, mix the remaining ¼ cup of Cheddar and bread crumbs in a small bowl. Sprinkle evenly over the macaroni and dot with the remaining 1 tablespoon of butter.

5. Bake for 20 minutes, or until the top bubbles and begins to form a crust.

Macaroni and cheese is so good that even Thomas Jefferson loved it. *Thomas Jefferson's Cook Book,* a collection of recipes used at Monticello, includes a recipe for macaroni baked with tons of melted cheese and butter. Legend has it that our third president invented the dish, but that's not quite right. He did, however, introduce pasta to the United States by having a macaroni machine sent over from Europe.

Of course, a lot of American history would roll by before the boxed version of this dinner would turn up on grocery store shelves. It was in 1937 that the Kraft Macaroni and Cheese Dinner was introduced. And it was marketed with the slogan: "Make a meal for 4 in 9 minutes." The need for quick meals is still a concern for modern families, but our recipe is more about creamy, triple-cheese deliciousness than speed, an emphasis that would surely have pleased President Jefferson.

three-bean vegetarian chili

Serves 8 to 10

When you sit down to this chili at the Comfort Diner, you get a bowl rimmed with tortilla chips. It's not uncommon to see people forgoing spoons altogether and scooping up the chili with the chips instead. Just be sure to get a bite of everything on each chip.

This recipe contains chocolate chips, a quirky addition that usually elicits surprise. The chocolate provides a real richness to the sauce. It was suggested by a line cook from Mexico as a riff on a traditional mole sauce.

3 tablespoons olive oil

2 cups small-diced carrots (2 to 3 medium-sized carrots)

1 cup small-diced green bell pepper (1 pepper)

2 cups small-diced red bell pepper (2 peppers)

1 jalapeño, sliced into thin circles

3 tablespoons chopped fresh cilantro

3 garlic cloves, minced

2 cups small-diced onions (2 medium-sized onions)

¼ cup ground cumin

3 tablespoons chili powder

1½ tablespoons freshly ground black pepper

1 teaspoon salt

2 cups Lively Tomato salsa (page 121), plus ½ cup for serving

4 cups chopped plum tomatoes (2 16-ounce cans)

2 cups canned white beans, drained (from 2 15-ounce cans)

2 cups canned black beans, drained (from 2 15-ounce cans)

2 cups canned kidney beans, drained (from 2 15-ounce cans)

½ cup chocolate chips

Tortilla chips

1 cup sour cream

1 cup (4 ounces) shredded Cheddar cheese

1. In a stockpot, heat the oil over medium heat. Sauté the carrots, bell peppers, jalapeño, cilantro, garlic, and onions for about 10 minutes, until the vegetables soften.

2. Add the cumin, chili powder, black pepper, and salt. Stir to combine. Add the 2 cups salsa, the canned plum tomatoes, white beans, black beans, kidney beans, and chocolate chips.

3. Bring to a boil. Reduce to a simmer and cook for about 45 minutes, until thick, adding up to ½ cup water as necessary while the chili cooks to prevent the chili from scorching.

4. Serve with tortilla chips, sour cream, salsa, and Cheddar on top.

pork chops *and* applesauce

Serves 4

Like diners of yore, we offer a different Blue Plate Special every day of the week. Pork Chops and Applesauce has been our Thursday night offering since we first opened, and it is the most popular of all the specials. *Brady Bunch* fans always get a kick when I deliver the line "Today's Blue Plate Special is Pork Chops and Applesauce" in that very Brady way. (À la episode #55, "The Personality Kid." Yep, I looked it up.)

½ cup olive oil

1 tablespoon chopped fresh thyme

1 teaspoon chopped fresh rosemary

2 tablespoons finely chopped shallot (1 large shallot)

2 garlic cloves, minced

¼ teaspoon salt

¼ teaspoon freshly ground black pepper

8 1-inch-thick double-cut pork loin chops (bone in)

Thick-N-Chunky Applesauce, to serve (page 110)

1. In a small bowl, mix the olive oil, thyme, rosemary, shallot, garlic, salt, and pepper.

2. Place the pork chops in a glass bowl or baking dish. Pour the marinade over the chops. Refrigerate for at least 2 hours or overnight.

3. Remove the meat from the marinade and drain off the excess marinade.

4. On a grill pan or a sauté pan, sear the pork chops over medium-high heat for 8 to 10 minutes on each side, until browned and cooked through. Serve with Thick-N-Chunky Applesauce.

mom's meatloaf

On the Comfort Diner menu, this dish is listed as Mom's Meatloaf "on her best day." Frankly, I think even on her *very* best day, Mom's wasn't nearly this good. In fact, my mom's version of this diner classic frightened me as a youngster. In her effort to give her family a complete meal, she loaded the mixture with peas (a vegetable I hated), then decorated it by sticking potato wedges into the top like spikes. The whole thing looked like a spooky enchanted forest in a pan. It gave me nightmares. I worked hard to come up with a soothing, tasty recipe. Give this a try. You'll be in dreamland.

3 tablespoons olive oil

2 garlic cloves, minced

1 cup finely diced white onion (1 medium-sized onion)

1 cup finely diced celery (2 to 3 stalks)

1/4 cup finely diced green bell pepper (from 1 bell pepper)

1 tablespoon dried basil

1 tablespoon dried thyme

1 tablespoon dried oregano

2 large eggs

1 cup whole milk

1 cup plain whole oats

1 pound ground beef

1/2 pound ground veal

1/2 pound ground pork

1/2 tablespoon salt

1/2 tablespoon freshly ground black pepper

1/4 cup Worcestershire sauce

1/2 cup canned diced tomatoes, drained

1/2 cup ketchup or canned diced tomatoes, for topping

1. Preheat the oven to 325°F. In a large sauté pan on medium heat, warm the olive oil, then add the garlic, onion, celery, bell pepper, basil, thyme, and oregano. Sauté the vegetables for 3 to 4 minutes, until they begin to soften.

2. In a bowl, whisk together the eggs and milk. Add the oats.

3. In a large bowl, combine the meats well by hand. Season with the salt and pepper. Pour the liquid mixture over the blended meats and mix thoroughly to combine. Add the Worcestershire sauce, tomatoes, and sautéed vegetables. Mix well.

4. Place the mixture in a 9×12-inch baking dish, and form it into a long, rounded loaf. There should be at least 1 inch of space around the loaf to allow fat to run off.

5. Spread the ketchup or diced tomatoes evenly on top of the loaf, and bake for 50 to 60 minutes, until firm and cooked through.

6. Remove the meatloaf from the oven and allow to cool for 2 to 3 minutes before serving.

Meatloaf is a staple of our menu—and it's a reliable dinner

for home cooks all over this country. German immigrants who came to these shores brought with them a tradition of dishes based on ground meats, like hamburgers, sausages, and meatloaf. But like most culinary imports, over the generations, meatloaf has continued to evolve in America. Ask ten people about their meatloaf and you'll get ten different versions. Some people cover the top with bacon. Some put boiled eggs in the middle. Some wouldn't dream of adding ketchup to the top—though we happen to think that the acidic tang of the tomato enlivens the soft, richness of the meat.

No matter what you put in your meatloaf, be sure to save the leftovers. A hunk of meatloaf between two slices of bread makes for a heavenly sandwich.

A Time to Share

One great tradition in American life is bringing a casserole over to a neighbor in need. Know a family that just had a baby? Or someone who's going through a tough time? That's when "comfort food" is needed most. Any one of these easy-to-cart-around, wholesome entrees will do the trick.

Comforting Chicken Potpie (page 98)

Mom's Meatloaf (page 92)

Macaroni and Cheese (page 88)

Yankee Pot Roast (page 95)

Diner Trivia

Diners are part of American food culture, but they're also part of our movie culture. Diner scenes pop up all the time. They're where people meet their pals, discover that their dad was a nerd, or reclaim superhuman powers. And so to honor Hollywood's depiction of diners, here's a Top Ten list of movies with best diner scenes.

1. *When Harry Met Sally*
2. *Five Easy Pieces*
3. *Blues Brothers*
4. *Pulp Fiction*
5. *Alice Doesn't Live Here Anymore*
6. *Back to the Future*
7. *Road to Perdition*
8. *Urban Cowboy*
9. *Superman II*
10. *Diner*

yankee pot roast

Serves 6

I'll let you in on a little secret. This pot roast is so good that whenever I know it's in the oven — with all the vegetables and meat simmering away in the savory broth — I can't pass up the chance to check on the process and carefully scoop out a carrot or two. This pot roast is simply irresistible. I highly recommend adding more carrots and beef than the recipe says, since if you're a nibbler, this dish will have you opening the oven door and "testing" the whole batch before you know it.

3 to 4 pounds beef brisket

2 tablespoons rough chopped fresh sage (about 10 leaves)

8 sprigs rosemary

8 sprigs thyme

½ cup olive oil

4 garlic cloves, rough chopped

1¼ teaspoons salt

2 teaspoons freshly ground black pepper

2 medium carrots, sliced into ¼-inch rounds (about 2 cups)

5 to 6 celery stalks, sliced into ½ inch pieces (about 2 cups)

2 cups large-diced Spanish onion (2 medium-sized onions)

3 garlic cloves, minced

4 cups tomato puree (from 1 29-ounce can plus 1 8-ounce can)

4 cups beef or veal stock

2 bay leaves

6 new potatoes, quartered (unpeeled)

1. In a glass baking dish, combine the beef, sage, rosemary, thyme, ¼ cup olive oil, chopped garlic, ¼ teaspoon of the salt, and 1 teaspoon of the pepper. Marinate for at least 2 hours or overnight if time allows.

2. After the meat has been marinated, remove it to a large skillet on high heat. Cook for 5 minutes on each side, until lightly seared and browned. Set it aside on a platter.

3. Preheat the oven to 350°F. In a roasting pan placed across two burners, heat the remaining ¼ cup olive oil. Sauté the carrot, celery, onion, minced garlic, and the remaining 1 teaspoon salt and 1 teaspoon pepper for 10 minutes, until the onion is soft.

4. Add the meat to the vegetables. Pour the tomato puree and beef stock over the meat. Add the bay leaves and potatoes. Bring to a boil, then reduce to a simmer for 10 minutes.

5. Cover the pan with aluminum foil and place in the oven. Cook for 2 to 2½ hours, until the meat is tender and falls apart easily.

6. Remove the meat from the pan. Slice the meat, arrange the slices on a serving platter, and pour the broth and vegetables over the meat.

spinach *and* feta–stuffed fillet of sole

Serves 4

This dish was inspired by the simplicity of Greek diner food, but it's been reworked to Comfort Diner standards. In other diners you might see sautéed fish with a side of spinach, and maybe a salad sprinkled with feta. We say: roll it all up together — in a classy way. This dish is a refined entree for a romantic evening and also a clever way to get kids to eat spinach and fish. They'll never notice the nutrition under all the oozing, melted feta cheese.

3 tablespoons unsalted butter

2 10-ounce bags fresh spinach, stemmed and thoroughly washed

1/4 teaspoon salt

1/2 teaspoon freshly ground black pepper

1 cup (4 ounces) crumbled feta cheese

1 tablespoon dried oregano

1 tablespoon chopped fresh parsley

4 6-ounce sole fillets (tilapia or another firm white fish can be substituted)

1 lemon

2 tablespoons olive oil

2 tablespoons paprika

1. Preheat the oven to 375°F.

2. In a large sauté pan, melt 1 tablespoon of the butter and sauté the spinach until wilted. Season with 1/8 teaspoon of the salt and 1/4 teaspoon of the pepper. (If your pan isn't big enough to handle all that spinach, this can be done in batches, with more butter added as needed.) Drain away any accumulated liquid from the spinach.

3. In a medium bowl, toss the cooked spinach with the crumbled feta cheese, oregano, and parsley.

4. On a clean work surface, lay the fish fillets flat and season with the remaining 1/8 teaspoon salt and 1/4 teaspoon pepper. Cover each fillet with the spinach-feta filling. Starting with the narrow end of the fillet, roll the fish into a tight, round package (as you would a jelly roll). If needed, fasten with a toothpick.

5. Place the rolled and stuffed fillets in a baking dish. Just before cooking squeeze the lemon and drizzle olive oil over the fish, then sprinkle with the paprika.

6. Bake for about 8 minutes, until the fish is opaque and white. Cooking time will depend on the thickness of the fish, so check frequently. Serve right away, while the cheese is hot.

A Table for Two

Preparing a romantic dinner for two means getting everything taken care of in advance. You'll want time to sit down and talk, without the pressure of running around the kitchen. So here's a menu to try. You can plate the salads well in advance, then pop the sole in the oven just before you're ready to sit down. By the time you've eaten the salads, the fish will be ready to serve. And be sure to have two straws for the shake!

Chopped Health Salad (page 47)

Spinach and Feta–Stuffed Fillet of Sole (page 96) served with rice

One Black and White Milkshake (page 132) to share

Diner Trivia

What state has the most diners?

The answer is New Jersey. That's according to food historian Peter Genovese, author of *Jersey Diners*, who spent a year traveling to all of them. His research shows that there are diners in half of New Jersey's 567 municipalities. That's a lot of milkshakes.

comforting chicken potpie

Serves 6

One of my earliest food memories involves chicken potpie. I was about four years old, and my mother had just taken a potpie out of the oven to let it cool. My brother Jeff, age two at the time, decided to plunge his hand smack into the middle of the potpie. He was rushed to the emergency room, and when he returned home, his hand was wrapped in an enormous gauzy bandage. I was green with envy at the sight of his fascinating white mitten. Not only didn't I get one of those nifty mittens, dang, I didn't even get to eat the potpie!

At the restaurant, I started making this with a Cheddar spoonbread crust, just to elevate the concept a bit. But I soon discovered that people preferred the traditional crust. It just goes to show that for some dishes, there's nothing like the classic.

4 6- to 8-ounce chicken breasts

6 tablespoons unsalted butter

2 cups small-diced carrots (2 to 3 medium-sized carrots)

1 cup small-diced celery (2 to 3 stalks)

1 cup small-diced red onion (1 medium-sized onion)

2 cups medium-diced red potatoes (6 medium-sized potatoes)

¼ cup all-purpose flour

1 cup heavy cream

4 cups chicken stock, homemade or store-bought

Salt and ground white pepper to taste

1 cup frozen green peas

1 sheet frozen puff pastry, thawed

1. Preheat the oven to 350°F. Bring a large pot of water to a boil. Boil the chicken for 10 minutes, until cooked through. Be careful not to overcook the chicken, as it will be cooked more later.

2. While the chicken is cooking, melt 2 tablespoons of the butter in a large saucepan over medium heat, and sauté the carrots, celery, onion, and potatoes for 5 minutes. Again, be careful to avoid overcooking. Remove the vegetables from the pan and set them aside in a large bowl.

3. When the chicken has cooked, remove from the water and drain. Slice it into bite-sized pieces.

4. In a saucepan over medium heat, melt the remaining ¼ cup butter. Sprinkle the flour over the butter. Stir gently and frequently for 2 to 3 minutes, until the flour is absorbed and the bubbling mixture is lightly golden.

5. Add the heavy cream and chicken stock. Mix thoroughly. Simmer for 10 minutes, then add the chicken and the sautéed vegetables. Season with the salt and pepper and simmer for 20 minutes more. Pour the mixture into a 9-inch pie pan and add the frozen peas.

6. Roll out the puff pastry so it is 2 inches larger than the pie pan. Place it over the pan and tuck down the edges into the pan. Cut a few slits on the top of the pastry to allow steam to escape. Bake for about 40 minutes, until the crust is golden brown.

Ah, the savory pie. Though the English can take credit for hearty meat pies, it's actually the influence of German Pennsylvania Dutch immigrants in America that made the chicken potpie a staple of American cuisine. Regional differences result in various tops to the steamy chicken stew that lies beneath. Some cooks cover the chicken and vegetable mixture with dumplings or even noodles called potpie squares. The chicken potpie reached the diner menu in the Depression Era and made for a tasty, reliable Blue Plate Special. As for the commercial take on this dish, Swanson launched its first frozen potpie in 1951, just two years before the Swanson TV dinner came along.

a simple healthy chicken dish

Serves 4

At the Comfort Diner, we walk a fine line between traditional diner food and healthful food that fits with the lifestyles of our customers. We want the menu to offer plenty of calorie-laden, stick-to-your-ribs comfort food, balanced by just enough diet-friendly choices. My goal is for guests to be just as likely to order a nice healthful chicken dish as a mac and cheese — and for both to be equally enjoyable. This dish is one that helps us meet that goal.

At home, this can be a lightning quick week-night dinner. But if you have the time, marinate the chicken breasts with some olive oil, chopped garlic, and thyme before cooking. Marinating for as little as 15 minutes will add considerable flavor to the chicken.

2 cups uncooked rice

4 6- to 8-ounce chicken breasts

2 cups peeled, seeded, and sliced cucumber (2 cucumbers)

2 cups large-diced red onion (2 medium-sized onions)

8 fresh plum tomatoes, cut in 1/4-inch circles

2 cups julienned carrot (3 medium-sized carrots)

3 cups large-diced yellow squash (2 to 3 medium squash)

2 cups broccoli, cut into small florets (1 head broccoli)

1 1/4 cup Serious Soy Vinaigrette (page 127)

1. In a pot, combine the rice with 4 cups of water. Bring to a boil, then cover and simmer for 15 to 20 minutes. (Or cook rice according to package directions.)

2. Brush a grill pan with 2 tablespoons olive oil. (If using a sauté pan, coat the pan with 2 tablespoons of olive oil.) Bring the pan to medium high heat and cook two of the chicken breasts for 8 to 10 minutes per side, until golden brown. When cooked through, remove from the heat, slice into strips, and set aside. Repeat with the remaining olive oil and chicken breasts.

3. Place the cucumber, onion, tomato, carrot, yellow squash, and broccoli in a large pot and pour in the vinaigrette. Heat gently on low heat for 6 to 8 minutes, until the onion just begins to soften. The vegetables should be just barely cooked.

4. Serve in large bowls with rice on the bottom, vegetables in the middle, and chicken on top.

brinley's lemon chicken

Serves 4

This dish is named for my nine-year-old daughter, Brinley, who loves chicken piccata but cringes at capers. At home, I came up with a variation on chicken piccata that incorporates mushrooms, a vegetable she adores. As it turned out, I created a hit. It's become a family staple and a customer favorite. Try it for your pickiest eater, even if that happens to be yourself.

4 6- to 8-ounce chicken breasts

½ cup flour

½ teaspoon salt

½ teaspoon freshly ground black pepper

2 tablespoons unsalted butter

2 tablespoons olive oil

1¾ cups chicken stock, homemade or store-bought

¼ cup fresh lemon juice (about 3 lemons)

2 cups sliced fresh white mushrooms (about 8 mushrooms)

1. Preheat the oven to 250°F. Place the chicken breasts between 2 sheets of waxed paper and pound the chicken to a uniform thickness.

2. Pour the flour in a large bowl and season with ¼ teaspoon of the salt and ¼ teaspoon of the pepper. Dredge the chicken in the flour until coated. Shake off the excess.

3. In a large skillet on medium-high heat, melt 1 tablespoon of the butter and all of the olive oil. Add the chicken and sauté for 8 to 10 minutes on each side, until cooked through and golden brown. Remove the chicken to a casserole dish and keep warm.

4. Pour the stock and lemon juice into the skillet and raise the heat to high. Season with the remaining ¼ teaspoon salt and ¼ teaspoon pepper. Scrape the bottom of the pan with a spatula and boil for 3 to 4 minutes. Add the mushrooms to the pan and heat for 4 to 5 minutes, until the mushrooms are just cooked through.

5. Remove from the heat. Swirl in the remaining 1 tablespoon of butter. Pour the mushroom sauce over the chicken and serve.

honey-dipt southern-fried chicken strips

Serves 4

Confession time, again. We don't actually dip the chicken in honey. It's much more fun to get one of those cute honey bears and squeeze it all over the crispy chicken at the table. Truly finger-lickin' good!

1 cup buttermilk

1 tablespoon Lawry's Seasoned Salt

2 teaspoons Cajun spice mix (or Goya "Hot" Adobo seasoning)

4 6- to 8-ounce boneless chicken breasts, sliced into long strips

2 cups flour

½ teaspoon garlic powder

½ teaspoon onion powder

½ teaspoon ground white pepper

½ teaspoon salt

2 cups vegetable oil (canola preferred), or as needed

Honey bears, to serve

1. In a large bowl, mix the buttermilk with the Lawry's and Cajun spice mix. Soak the chicken in this mixture for 10 minutes.

2. In a separate bowl, combine the flour with the garlic powder, onion powder, white pepper, and salt. Dredge the marinated chicken in the flour mixture until completely covered.

3. Pour ¾ cup of the oil into a large stockpot or a cast-iron skillet. Raise the heat to medium high. Test the oil by placing one chicken strip in it. The oil should sizzle and cook the chicken immediately.

4. Place 4 to 5 chicken strips (or as many as will fit without touching each other) into the oil and fry for 7 to 8 minutes, until golden brown. Turn occasionally to prevent burning. When fully cooked, place the chicken strips on paper towels to blot excess oil before serving. Let the oil reheat and repeat the process with the remaining chicken. Replace the oil if it becomes too dark; the flour falling off from the chicken strips can stay in the oil and burn.

5. Serve the chicken strips with honey bears.

Honey tastes good no matter what its packaging, but somehow those squeezable bear-shaped containers make that golden liquid sugar all the more fun. The history of the honey bear dates back to 1957, when California beekeeper Woodrow Miller and his Pennsylvania distributor came up with the idea. There's no real reason why the containers took the bear shape (except that bears are cute and they love honey), and it took some time before a soft, squeezable plastic was created for easy use. No one ever filed a patent on the shape, but it was one good idea — those bears are darn handy: scooping honey out of a jar gets sticky, now, doesn't it?

Diner Trivia

From Atlantic City to San Francisco, the old Route 40 carried travelers directly across this great country. According to the Web site *www.route40.net*, there are 353 diners along the highway that in its heydey was 3,220 miles long. Of all the fourteen states the road cuts through, only the stretch in West Virginia does not have a diner on it.

chipotle-rubbed cowboy steak

Serves 4

This steak has a smokey, mildly spicy kick. That's because chipotle peppers are jalapeños that have been smoked. At the restaurant we use a chipotle powder, but if you can't find it, you can substitute a chipotle hot sauce to bring this wonderful flavor to the beef. If you were out on the range for months and rolled into a booth at the Comfort Diner, I'm sure you'd be one happy cowboy.

4 ¾-inch-thick strip, loin, or rib-eye steaks

½ cup olive oil

½ cup chipotle powder, or 1 cup chipotle-flavored sauce (such as Goya Salsita Hot Sauce)

¼ teaspoon freshly ground black pepper, or to taste

1. Rub each steak with the oil, chipotle powder, and pepper. Marinate for at least an hour.

2. Grill or broil steaks on high heat for 4 minutes on each side for medium-rare steaks, or for 6 minutes on each side for medium.

One Really Big Dinner

Need a no-nonsense meat-and-potatoes dinner to feed an unruly crowd of cowboys? Or maybe a wild pack of teenagers? Or just a bunch of really hungry people? Here's a stick-to-your-ribs dinner that will have 'em all stuffed to the gills—and napping in no time. And you can change the name of the dessert to suit your needs. Why not the Wild West Coffee Cake?

Roasted Garlic Mashed Potatoes (page 114)

Cowboy Baked Beans (page 112)

Chicken Fried Steak (page 105)

Russian Coffee Cake (page 150)

chicken fried steak

Serves 4

Why batter-fry beef? C'mon! Everybody loves that crunch. And this way there are no chicken bones to mess with. Sometimes we substitute a chicken breast for the beef and serve Chicken Fried Chicken. Try it both ways.

8 ⅛-inch-thick, top round beef cutlets

5 large eggs

4 cups all-purpose flour

1 tablespoon Lawry's Seasoned Salt

3 cups vegetable oil (canola preferred), or as needed

1. Place the beef between 2 sheets of waxed paper and pound to an even thickness. (The cutlets should be very thin sliced already. This step will ensure that they are even.)

2. Beat the eggs in a bowl and set aside. Combine the flour and Lawry's Seasoned Salt in another bowl. Dredge the cutlets in the flour, then dip them in the egg. Dredge in the flour again.

3. Pour ¾ cup of the oil into a large stockpot or a cast-iron skillet, and raise the heat to medium high.

4. Gently place 1 cutlet in the hot oil. The oil should sizzle and cook the beef immediately. Cook for 2 to 3 minutes, until the breading is set and golden brown. Turn with a long-handled meat fork or tongs. Cook for another 2 to 3 minutes, until golden brown. Repeat with the remaining cutlets.

5. Remove the cutlets from the skillet and drain on a platter lined with paper towels. Let the oil reheat and repeat the process with the remaining cutlets. Replace the oil if it becomes too dark; the flour falling off the beef can stay in the oil and burn. Serve immediately.

"Do you want to share?"

chapter 7

side dishes

Culinary Sidecars

Sometimes, you gotta choose sides. But when it's time to pick between Thick-N-Chunky Applesauce and Colorful Coleslaw, every choice is a winner.

Side dishes aren't meant to get top billing, but they're the must-have additions that enhance the main event. And they are certainly not to be taken for granted. Doesn't a good steak taste even better with a side of creamed spinach? Where would pork chops or potato pancakes be without sweet applesauce to bring out the full flavor? As for tortilla chips, they're just dry flaky triangles if they don't have a bowlful of fresh salsa nearby.

If you're going to a dinner party or a potluck supper, side dishes can be the perfect items to bring. They're quick to make and don't steal anyone's thunder, but they add immeasurably to the enjoyment of what's on offer. And if you've got guests coming over, you can plan the preparations so that a busybody friend can be "in charge" of a side dish. When he or she asks, "How can I help?" you'll have an answer—and some fresh coleslaw to boot.

colorful coleslaw

Serves 6

I decided to put apples and raisins into our coleslaw for two reasons. First, it just tastes good. Second, they make it clear that it's homemade — or at least Comfort Diner made. After you taste this, you'll never again be satisfied with that limp, overcreamy coleslaw from the deli.

4 cups shredded or thin-sliced green cabbage (½ head of cabbage)

1 cup shredded carrots (2 medium-sized carrots)

½ cup raisins

2 cups finely diced Granny Smith apple (1 unpeeled apple)

¼ cup mayonnaise (or more if preferred)

1 tablespoon sugar

Salt to taste

1. In a large bowl, toss together the cabbage, carrots, raisins, and apple.

2. Mix in the mayonnaise until the vegetables are evenly coated.

3. Sprinkle in the sugar. Toss again to combine. Season lightly with salt.

Diner Trivia

If this book gives you the urge to set up your very own diner, you've got plenty of resources. There are still companies that manufacture diners and will put them up where ever you like. Kullman Industries of Lebanon, New Jersey, has been building diners (and other modular structures) since 1927. Valiant Diners of Ormond Beach, Florida, can build you a stainless steel wonder that seats sixty to two hundred people. As can Dinermite Diners of Atlanta, Georgia, which has been building since the 1960s.

If you were to compare our recipe for Colorful Coleslaw
with a recipe for a Waldorf salad, you might think that there's a lot in common. And you'd be right. There is. But the Waldorf salad was around for a hundred years before the Comfort Diner opened in 1996. Really. The recipe appeared in the Waldorf-Astoria hotel's cookbook, published in 1896.

The Waldorf salad—which originally contained only apples, celery, and mayonnaise—was created by the hotel's legendary maître d', Oscar Tschirky. Walnuts were later added to the mix. (The Switzerland-born Tschirky, by the way, is also credited with having created Thousand Island dressing.)

The primary ingredient in our diner slaw, by contrast, is cabbage. The raisins, apples, and carrots are the accents that enliven the dish and add a little crunch. You could add walnuts, too, if you like. And you could mix in golden raisins with brown ones.

thick-n-chunky applesauce

Serves 6 to 8

Here's a recipe that I've changed a bit to make things easier on cooks at home. At the diner, our applesauce is made from apples chopped into ¼-inch dice, then cooked down. And if you have the time to slice and dice, be my guest. But this side dish is just as good if you use an apple corer/slicer to divide the fruit into eighths. Give yourself a break — I'm sure you deserve it.

Be sure to avoid using Macintosh or red delicious apples to make applesauce — when cooked, they become too soft to yield the right chunky texture.

6 Granny Smith apples (unpeeled)

¼ cup raisins (optional)

1½ cups orange juice

¼ cup packed brown sugar

⅛ teaspoon ground cloves (from 2 cloves)

1 cinnamon stick

1 dash ground nutmeg

1 dash ground allspice

1. Slice the apples into eighths using an apple corer/slicer or simply core the apples and cut into thick wedges.

2. Place the apples in a stockpot. Add the raisins, orange juice, brown sugar, cloves, cinnamon stick, nutmeg, and allspice.

3. Bring to a boil, then remove the cinnamon stick. Simmer until the apples are soft enough to mash, about 30 minutes.

4. Break up the apples with a masher or large fork. The consistency should be thick, but not uniform.

While apple growers suggest several different varieties of apples for making applesauce, among the most popular is the bright green Granny Smith.

Now with stories about Johnny Appleseed and old saws like "as American as apple pie" floating around, it's easy to think that apples are a red-white-and-blue original. But Granny Smith apples originated in Australia. They're named for "Granny" Maria Ann Smith of Ryde, New South Wales, who with her husband, Thomas, was a fruit grower. In the late 1860s, she discovered an apple tree growing by a creek on her farm and showed it to a neighbor. The variety was not commercially marketed when Smith was living, but it was later cultivated by local farmers and the Granny Smith name stuck.

Everything's Comin' up Carbs

Gave up carbohydrates? Sure you did. And so now you're back. From outer space. And you've got that look upon your face — the one that says, I need carbs NOW! No problem. Here's the "Welcome Back" dinner. Guaranteed to reverse all the effects of your low-carb diet in a single meal.

cowboy baked beans

Serves 4

This is a simple way to give some kick to your average canned baked beans. There's just enough spice here to make you feel like a cowboy on the western plains. You can serve these beside steaks, burgers, hot dogs, or just about any hearty grub you like. Add some mashed potatoes and you're eatin' hearty.

3 strips bacon

3 tablespoons vegetable oil

1 cup small-diced onion (1 medium-sized onion)

1 28-ounce can baked beans

1 tablespoon brown sugar

1 tablespoon ketchup

1½ tablespoons chili powder

1. Cook the bacon until it is crispy using your preferred method.

2. In a sauté pan, warm the oil over medium heat. Add the onion and sauté for 3 to 4 minutes, until it begins to soften. Add the bacon and cook for 2 minutes more.

3. Add the baked beans, brown sugar, ketchup, and chili powder. Heat for 5 minutes, stirring frequently.

creamed spinach

This is a decadent side dish that gets people reaching and throwing elbows at a dinner table — like basketball players looking for the rebound. But the best part is the dish can be done in just a little more time than it takes for the spinach to wilt.

1 10-ounce bag spinach

½ cup heavy cream

¼ cup cream cheese, cubed

1 tablespoon unsalted butter

Salt and freshly ground black pepper to taste

1. Remove any stems from the spinach and be sure that it is thoroughly washed and drained.

2. In a large saucepan over medium-low heat, gently warm the heavy cream and cream cheese.

3. When the cream cheese has melted, add the spinach. Heat for 5 to 6 minutes, until the spinach has wilted and the cream begins to simmer. Stir in the butter and season with salt and pepper. Serve right away.

Diner Trivia

Television has been just as friendly to diners as film. On *Beverly Hills 90210,* the teens hung out at the Peach Pit, a retro-50s joint. Al's Diner on *Happy Days* looked a bit like a paneled basement, but still had the milkshakes to back it up. The cast of *Seinfeld* referred to Monk's Diner as a coffee shop, but that's common parlance in New York City, where block-long diners are rare. The entire show *Alice* was based in Mel's Diner. And *Twin Peaks* stayed true to reality by filming scenes at Twede's Café, built in 1941 and still serving "A damn fine cup o' coffee!"

roasted garlic mashed potatoes

Mashed potatoes are one of the ultimate original comfort foods. People come in the restaurant just for mashed potatoes to go. But as you'll see in this recipe, they're easy enough to do at home. (And for some reason, I've found that pregnant women love these mashed potatoes!)

1 head garlic

12 medium-sized new potatoes

¼ cup (½ stick) butter

½ cup heavy cream

¼ cup whole milk

Salt and freshly ground black pepper to taste

1. Preheat the oven to 350°F. Slice the papery tuft off the garlic head and place the garlic head in a baking dish. Roast the garlic in the oven for 30 to 40 minutes (depending on size), until the cloves are soft and mashable.

2. Meanwhile, place the potatoes in a large pot of water and bring to a boil. Cook the potatoes for about 25 to 30 minutes, until soft. Drain the potatoes and place in a mixing bowl.

3. Remove the roasted garlic from the oven. When it is cool to the touch, slip each clove from its papery layer and add it to the potatoes.

4. In a saucepan over low heat, melt the butter, then add the cream and milk. Heat until just warm. Do not boil.

5. Gradually pour the liquid over the potatoes, and mix using a hand-mixer or masher, until the potatoes are creamy and thoroughly blended. Season with salt and pepper.

sweet potato mashed potatoes

Serves 6 to 8

Sweet potatoes are loaded with vitamins A and C, and they're a flavorful way to bring some color to your meals. This recipe includes a few white potatoes so that you don't wind up with a pool of runny sweet potato puree. If you're not sure what to serve these with, just think of any meat or poultry dish that you would serve with mashed potatoes — and then serve these instead.

4 sweet potatoes, peeled

2 Idaho potatoes, peeled

½ cup heavy cream

½ cup whole milk

¼ cup (½ stick) butter, melted

Pinch of ground nutmeg

Salt and freshly ground black pepper to taste

1. Place the sweet potatoes in a large pot and cover with water. Bring to a boil and cook for 30 minutes, until soft. Place the Idaho potatoes in a separate large pot and cover with water. Bring to a boil and cook for 30 to 40 minutes, until soft.

2. Drain the potatoes and place them together in a large mixing bowl.

3. Add the cream, milk, butter, and nutmeg. Using a hand-mixer, whip the potatoes until thick, creamy, and thoroughly blended with the liquids. (If you don't have a handheld mixer, a potato masher will do.) Season with salt and pepper.

not-fried fries

Serves 4 to 6

At the Comfort Diner, we serve two kinds of French fries (sweet potato and regular), but I know what it's like to make dinner at home. No one really wants to get out the deep-fat frier just for a side dish. So I've adapted our French fry recipe into a home-friendly method. These baked potato wedges can be served with almost anything—from a hamburger to an omelet. And the seasoning is just a starting point, so feel free to sprinkle your spuds with whatever you like.

4 to 5 Idaho potatoes, cut into long, ½-inch-thick wedges

¼ cup vegetable oil

1 teaspoon salt, or to taste

1 teaspoon freshly ground black pepper

½ tablespoon paprika

1. Preheat the oven to 350°F. Toss the potatoes with the oil, salt, pepper, and paprika.

2. On two cookie sheets or in two 9×12-inch baking dishes, spread out the potatoes in a single layer. (If you don't have a second baking dish or baking sheet, you can bake these in batches.)

3. Roast in the oven for 30 to 35 minutes, until tender and golden brown.

French fries are a necessary part of diner fare, and though the name suggests a Gallic origin, they may very well have originated in the good ol' U.S. of A. The term *French* was applied to describe the method of cutting the potatoes in thin strips: frenching.

As you can see from our recipe, you need not fry potatoes at home when you want a finger-food side dish. The slice-and-bake method will save you a lot of hassle. And if you feel like getting creative with the seasoning, there are lots of ways to add some variety. After tossing the potatoes in a little oil, give these sprinkles a try, then continue to follow the recipe. Let your tastes be the guide to the quantities of seasoning you use.

Old Bay Seafood Seasoning

Parmesan cheese and dried parsley

Garlic salt and oregano

Cajun seasoning

Chili powder, cumin, and black pepper

Fresh rosemary and sea salt

Black sesame seeds mixed with sea salt

Citrus-flavored salt

"Needs more mustard"

chapter 8

clever condiments and
dashing dressings

Very Dear Schmears

At the Comfort Diner, it's a point of pride that our condiments are made on site. We don't get big vats of tartar sauce delivered to our door. We don't order our salad dressings from a food service distributor. We make them ourselves. We even spice up our own mustard. And it's been that way since we opened our doors.

So pardon me if I brag just a bit about the work the Comfort Diner staff puts into the little extras. It's entirely justifiable. And I promise that when you start to make your own condiments, you'll feel the same about your creations. When someone asks you about that delicious cocktail sauce, you'll see what I mean. To be able to say "I made it" is a wonderful feeling. I hope you'll have the chance to enjoy that feeling often. I know that these days everyone is short on time, but when it comes to feeding your friends and family, why not go the extra mile? As with side dishes, condiments are a great way to include guests or children in the cooking process. And they'll add an extra layer of homestyle flavor that'll make your food truly comforting.

honey mustard dressing

Makes ¹/₂ cup

Here's a little restaurant secret. On every table at the Comfort Diner is a jar of our house-blend mustard. We make it our way by adding in a little horseradish with straight mustard for some extra "oomph." Try mixing up your own at home if you can't find a mustard that lights your world — or your nasal passages — on fire. I recommend starting with any smooth deli-style mustard, not a Dijon. But remember: every brand of mustard and every style of horseradish will yield a different result.

Our spicy mustard is also the base for our Honey Mustard Dressing. We mix in the honey to create that sweet-and-sour dressing that people just can't seem to get enough of. When you transform your own mustard into Honey Mustard Dressing, you may need to use more or less honey to get that perfect balance of heat and sweet. Use this recipe as a starting point, and tinker until you're satisfied.

2 tablespoons horseradish, drained of liquid

¼ cup smooth deli-style mustard

2 tablespoons honey

In a small mixing bowl, combine all of the ingredients thoroughly. To store, keep in a tightly sealed, refrigerated container for up to 3 weeks.

lively tomato salsa

Makes 4 cups

This is one of the most versatile condiments we serve. Make a big batch and serve it with tortilla chips, salads, eggs, or our Three-Bean Vegetarian Chili (page 90). You can also use it any time you would use ketchup. (Sounds crafty, huh?)

3½ cups chopped plum tomatoes (about 6 tomatoes)

1 cup finely diced red onion (1 medium-sized onion)

1 garlic clove, minced

2 jalapeño peppers (more or less, if preferred), seeded and minced

¼ cup chopped fresh cilantro

2 tablespoons lime juice (from 1–2 limes)

Salt and freshly ground black pepper to taste

In a large bowl, combine the tomatoes, onion, garlic, and jalapeño. Toss with the cilantro and lime juice. Season with salt and pepper. To store, keep in a tightly sealed, refrigerated container for up to 1 week.

Diner Trivia

In the 1930s, diners were designed to look more and more like streamlined railcars, and style became of increasing importance. On the exteriors, instead of boxy edges, diners began to have curved metal corners and a fin on the top. Inside, surfaces like tile, ceramic, and wood gave way to shiny materials like stainless steel, glass, and formica. The latter was created in the late 1930s and was first used in industrial settings as insulation, in place of mica. And from that came the name *for mica*. The slick, indestructable material was soon available in a variety of colors and designs. And would soon take over home kitchens, too.

SAVE STEPS, TIME and TIRES

It's not quite "The Thrilla in Manila," but there is a battle royale between ketchup and salsa. In the mid-1990s salsa sales outpaced ketchup, but the trend was later reversed. It may very well be reversed again in the future depending on food trends and which way the wind blows.

If the contest was based on history, ketchup would surely win. The origins of this condiment go all the way back to Chinese fish sauce that English sailors brought home with them in the seventeenth century. Tomato-based ketchup in bottles began to be sold in the United States in the mid nineteenth century. Heinz was selling it in 1876.

Salsa, by contrast, is a relative newcomer on the American food scene. A typical element of Mexican-American cuisine, it has taken hold as large numbers of Hispanic immigrants have come north. Salsa can be freshly made at home, freshly packaged, or trapped for dear life in jars in the form of runny soup. I think you know where our preferences lie (page 121).

your very own tartar sauce

Makes 1/2 cup

When you start making your own condiments, it's hard to go back to the store-bought, preservative-laden kind. And that's especially true with tartar sauce. You can whip this up just minutes before serving your favorite fish recipes. If you have some left over, add a dollop of ketchup and you've got Your Very Own Thousand Island Dressing.

3 tablespoons minced sweet pickles

1/3 cup mayonnaise

1/2 tablespoon lemon juice

1/4 teaspoon Worcestershire sauce

In a small mixing bowl, combine all of the ingredients thoroughly. To store, keep in a tightly sealed, refrigerated container for up to 1 week.

tangy remoulade sauce

Makes 1½ cups

This tangy sauce complements our Rhode Island Clam Fritters (page 39), Crab Burgers (page 66), or just plain crab cakes (that's the burger, without the bun). Make it with a good, strong mustard and you'll have a refreshing alternative to tartar sauce for any seafood dish.

½ cup prepared horseradish, drained of liquid

½ cup coarse-grain mustard

½ cup mayonnaise

½ cup finely diced shallots (4 shallots)

1 tablespoon finely chopped chives

1 tablespoon lemon juice

3 dashes Tabasco sauce (more or less as preferred)

Salt and ground white pepper to taste

1. Mix the horseradish, mustard, and mayonnaise in a medium bowl. Add shallots and chives and mix.

2. Add the lemon juice and Tabasco. Season with salt and pepper. Keep refrigerated until ready to serve. To store, keep in a tightly sealed, refrigerated container for up to 1 week.

cranberry sauce

Makes 2 cups

When I was eleven years old, my grade-school class went on a trip to Cape Cod. I was completely fascinated by the cranberry bogs. What eleven-year-old wouldn't be? And there I had a revelation: cranberries don't grow in the shape of tin cans! Nope, they're *berries*. That's big news when you're eleven. And now that I'm ever so slightly older, I still just won't eat the jiggly cranberry stuff from a can. Not when the fresh version takes less time to cook than watching one episode of *Happy Days*.

3 cups cranberries, from one 12-ounce bag

1½ cups orange juice

¼ cup packed brown sugar

1. In a saucepan, combine the cranberries, orange juice, and brown sugar.

2. Bring to a boil, then reduce the heat and simmer for 20 to 25 minutes, until the cranberries have softened and the consistency is thick. To store, keep in a tightly sealed, refrigerated container for up to 3 weeks.

balsamic vinaigrette

Makes ³/₄ cup

This is hands-down our most popular dressing. It's so popular we've started to bottle and sell it. It's just right with almost any leafy green salad you can think of. What makes it so good? For one thing, there's a lot more than just oil and vinegar — shallots and honey really round out the flavor. Second, we put it in the food processor so the texture is smooth, creamy, and held together. You can mix by hand if you like, but you gotta give it some elbow grease. Which you'll find in the frozen food section. (Just kidding.)

3 tablespoons balsamic vinegar

2 tablespoons chopped shallots
  (about 2 shallots)

1 tablespoon Dijon mustard

1 tablespoon honey

½ cup olive oil

Salt and freshly ground black pepper to taste

1. Place the vinegar, shallots, mustard, and honey in the bowl of a food processor.

2. With the motor running, add the oil in a steady stream and blend until thick and creamy, not separated. Season to taste. To store, keep in a tightly sealed, refrigerated container for up to 3 weeks.

serious soy vinaigrette

Makes 1¼ cups

This one packs a punch, oh yes, it does. This recipe is good for anyone who wants a lot of flavor from a dressing, but doesn't want the fats from oil or mayonnaise.

½ cup smooth Dijon mustard

½ cup soy sauce

¼ cup lemon juice (about 3 lemons)

1. In a large bowl, mix the mustard and soy sauce thoroughly.

2. Add lemon juice and stir to combine. To store, keep in a tightly sealed, refrigerated container for up to 3 weeks.

Diner Trivia

Even in the years of the Depression, diners were still viable businesses. They served wholesome food at low prices—and everybody still had to eat. But after surviving that and changing with the times, diners saw a new wrinkle in their business plans: McDonalds. In 1954, Ray Kroc—a distributor of milkshake machines—went to visit a hamburger stand run by Dick and Mac McDonald, who had just bought a large number of machines. People were lined up for the inexpensive burgers, which the cooks turned out as if they were on an assembly line. Kroc convinced the brothers to franchise, and by 1962 the company was running national advertisements. To compete with fast food, diners began presenting themselves as family restaurants and offered more selection.

creamy caesar salad dressing

Makes 1 cup

I like dressings thick and creamy — even Caesar dressing. So that's the way we do it. We don't add the raw egg because customers are always asking about it. The recipe works well without it, so save yourself the worry.

2 tablespoons smooth Dijon mustard

1 tablespoon red wine vinegar

5 canned anchovies

3 garlic cloves, roughly chopped

1 cup grated Parmesan cheese

2 tablespoons Worcestershire sauce

¼ cup lemon juice (about 3 lemons)

1 teaspoon salt

1 teaspoon freshly ground black pepper

½ cup olive oil

1. In the bowl of a food processor, combine the mustard, vinegar, anchovies, garlic, and Parmesan cheese. Mix for a few seconds to combine.

2. Add the Worcestershire sauce, lemon juice, salt, and pepper to the food processor. With the motor running, add the olive oil in a steady stream. The dressing should be thick and creamy. Chill to prevent separation. To store, keep in a tightly sealed, refrigerated container for up to 2 weeks.

blue cheese dressing

Makes 3 cups

I know, I know. Why bother making blue cheese dressing at home, when it's so easy to buy a bottle? Well, because this is lip-smackin', finger-lickin' good, that's why. Start with a fresh wedge of Maytag blue cheese and crumble it yourself. Try to avoid buying the precrumbled, prepackaged variety — it just doesn't have that bite.

This recipe makes a larger portion than most of the other dressings — and for a good reason. If you're making the Buffalo Wings (page 32), you'll need a hefty portion of it on the table. Use the leftovers (if you have any) as a salad dressing or with the Cobb Salad Sandwich (page 60).

1 cup mayonnaise

½ cup sour cream

½ cup buttermilk

¼ cup grated Parmesan cheese

3 tablespoons Worcestershire sauce

3 dashes Tabasco sauce

¾ pound Maytag blue cheese, or other quality blue cheese

Salt and freshly ground black pepper to taste

1. In the bowl of a food processor, combine the mayonnaise, sour cream, buttermilk, Parmesan cheese, Worcestershire sauce, and Tabasco. Blend to combine.

2. Pour the dressing into a bowl and crumble the blue cheese into the dressing by hand. Using a wooden spoon, mix gently. The dressing should be creamy, with the cheese evenly blended in. Season with salt and pepper. To store, keep in a tightly sealed, refrigerated container for up to 1 week.

"Extra Thick? U-Bet!"

chapter 9

milkshake mania

Smooth, Creamy, Cold, and Delicious

It's hard to know what's best. Is it the first sip of a cold milkshake that floods the senses and gives you a shiver of relief? Is it the gulp of milkshake in between a bite of a meaty cheeseburger and a handful of salty French fries? Or is it that last blob of ice cream that slides slowly out of the stainless steel milkshake container holding the overflow?

No matter what gives you a charge, a milkshake is a true pleasure—and a distinctly American one at that. From drive-in movie theaters to twenty-four-hour diners, milkshakes represent innocent, good times. They're the stuff of carefree teenagers cruising around on a hot summer night, or of little kids begging their parents for a trip to the ice cream parlor. The American fascination with ice cream plus milk and syrup is reinforced in movies and television, but it's also passed down to each generation. Stop by any local ice cream shop on a weekend night, and there's most likely a line out the door.

Take my word for it—we love milkshakes at the Comfort Diner. In fact, we love them so much that we made the world's largest milkshake. It was a 6,000 gallon concoction (a Black and White shake) and is listed in the *Guinness Book of World Records*. And if you love them, too, the next few pages are going to make you giddy.

black *and* white milkshake

Here you have the all-time classic, the Grand-Poobah, the mac-daddy of milk-shakes. But this recipe is just the tip of the ice(cream)berg. Every August is Milkshake Month at the Comfort Diner. We offer a different specialty milkshake every day. They get a little silly, but that's what we're all about. You'll see.

3 large scoops vanilla ice cream

3 tablespoons chocolate syrup (Fox's U-Bet preferred)

¼ cup whole milk

1. In the cup of a milkshake mixer or the pitcher of a blender, combine the ice cream, syrup, and milk.

2. Blend for 3 minutes in a milkshake mixer or 1 to 1½ minutes in a blender. The milkshake should be so thick that a straw stands up on its own in the middle of the shake.

When you're making a chocolate or black-and-white milkshake, take care in picking your chocolate syrup. At the Comfort Diner, we use Fox's U-Bet, a rich syrup with a distinctive chocolate flavor. The company behind this sweet stuff, H. Fox & Co., has been manufacturing for more than a hundred years and is still based in Brooklyn, New York.

Fox's U-Bet is also the main ingredient of another classic diner beverage: the egg cream. The creator of that treat was Louis Auster, a Jewish immigrant who operated soda fountains on Manhattan's Lower East Side. Despite the name, there are neither eggs nor cream in this treat. Just syrup, milk, and a squirt of seltzer. When everything is blended properly, the carbonated water makes the milk foam up. Originally, Auster made his own chocolate syrup. But when he died, he took the recipe with him, and Fox's U-Bet became the syrup of choice.

creamsicle milkshake

Serves 1

This tastes just like that orange-y ice cream bar you loved when you were a kid. When I watch customers try this shake, I can practically see one of those cartoon-thought bubbles over their heads: "It's the Creamsicle . . . from the ice cream man!"

2 large scoops vanilla ice cream

1 large scoop orange sherbert

½ cup orange juice

1. In the cup of a milkshake mixer or the pitcher of a blender, combine the ice cream, sherbet, and orange juice.

2. Blend for 3 minutes in a milkshake mixer or 1 to 1½ minutes in a blender. The milkshake should be so thick that a straw stands up on its own in the middle of the shake.

The Speedy Dinner

Everybody needs that one go-to menu to rely on when you get home from work and need a fast dinner. The creamed spinach takes almost no time to cook. And the vegetables in the chicken dish are just barely cooked. Start the prep by sautéing the chicken and you can almost have this whole dinner ready in the time it takes the chicken to cook.

A Simple Healthy Chicken Dish (page 100)

Creamed Spinach (page 113)

Cookies and Cream Milkshake (page 135)

cookies *and* cream milkshake

Serves 1

Are you a control freak? Then this is the milkshake for you. You can manage the cookie-to-ice-cream ratio exactly as you want it. Just get some Oreo cookies, mash 'em, and toss those bits of cookies and cream into your milkshake. At the restaurant, we use cookies and cream ice cream, but mashing up a bunch of cookies is a lot more fun.

3 large scoops cookies and cream ice cream (or
   3 scoops vanilla ice cream and 6 Oreo cookies,
   slightly crumbled by hand)

1/4 cup whole milk

1. In the cup of a milkshake mixer or the pitcher of a blender, combine the ice cream, cookies, if using, and milk.

2. Blend for 3 minutes in a milkshake mixer or 1 to 1½ minutes in a blender. The milkshake should be so thick that a straw stands up on its own in the middle of the shake.

When Nabisco introduced the Oreo cookie in 1912, the company quickly discovered that it had a winner on its hands. The Oreo has enjoyed many years reigning as America's best-selling cookie. Though the cookies have stayed pretty much true to their original shape and taste over the years, all sorts of variations on the theme have come to market. In 1975 the Double Stuf Oreo hit the shelves. In the 1980s, fudge-covered Oreos and Cookies N Cream ice cream extended the brand further. Things got cute and colorful in the 1990s: Mini Oreos were introduced, as well as seasonal versions, with orange cream for Halloween, red for Christmas, blue for spring. And don't forget Oreo O's cereal, Reduced Fat Oreos, and Double Delight Oreos, which feature two creams like peanut butter and chocolate in the same cookie. Hey, there's something for everyone.

the elvis milkshake

Elvis's favorite sandwich was peanut butter and banana. So in honor of The King, we've created a milkshake that combines vanilla ice cream with a scoop of peanut butter and a banana. We like to joke that for the young Elvis, we use smooth peanut butter. And for the older Elvis, well, we use chunky. So take your pick — and increase the amount of peanut butter if you really love the nutty stuff.

3 tablespoons peanut butter

3 large scoops vanilla ice cream

1 whole banana

½ cup whole milk

1. Heat the peanut butter in the microwave for 30 seconds. This will allow the peanut butter to blend into the milkshake properly.

2. In the cup of a milkshake mixer or the pitcher of a blender, combine the ice cream, peanut butter, banana, and milk.

3. Blend for 3 minutes in a milkshake mixer or 1 to 1½ minutes in a blender. The milkshake should be so thick that a straw stands up on its own in the middle of the shake.

mochachino milkshake

It's the middle of the afternoon. You've got the 3:00 p.m. doldrums. But if you have one of these, you're gonna be buzzing for the rest of the day. The sugar and espresso will get you out wheelin' and dealin' in no time.

3 large scoops vanilla ice cream

1 shot espresso, chilled

¼ cup whole milk

2 tablespoons chocolate syrup (Fox's U-Bet preferred)

1. In the cup of a milkshake mixer or the pitcher of a blender, combine the ice cream, espresso, milk, and syrup.

2. Blend for 3 minutes in a milkshake mixer or 1 to 1½ minutes in a blender. The milkshake should be so thick that a straw stands up on its own in the middle of the shake.

piña colada milkshake

Serves 1

This is one of our F.A.O. milkshakes — "For Adults Only." That's because there's a little shot of rum in this milkshake, which makes grown-up time a little more fun.

1 scoop pineapple sorbet

2 scoops coconut ice cream

¼ cup pineapple juice

1 jigger rum

1. In the cup of a milkshake mixer or the pitcher of a blender, combine the sorbet, ice cream, juice, and rum.

2. Blend for 3 minutes in a milkshake mixer or 1 to 1½ minutes in a blender. The milkshake should be so thick that a straw stands up on its own in the middle of the shake.

Diner Trivia

If you want to learn more about diners and their history, the American Diner Museum can help. Since 1996 it has worked to preserve the history and culture of this American original. The museum's permanent home will soon be in Providence, Rhode Island, the birthplace of the diner. For now, its Web site, www.dinermuseum.org, is packed with information about diners, including a diner locator. So you won't have to go hungry, no matter where your travels take you.

s'mores milkshake

Serves 1

We've got one super gooey milkshake here. And with the combination of Marsh-mallow Fluff, crumbled graham cracker, and chocolate ice cream, I think this is almost better than the campfire favorite. Go ahead and add chocolate chips if you like.

1/4 cup whipped marshmallow cream

3 large scoops chocolate ice cream

2 graham crackers

1/4 cup whole milk

1. Heat the marshmallow cream in the microwave for 30 seconds. This will allow the marshmallow cream to blend into the milkshake properly.

2. In the cup of a milkshake mixer or the pitcher of a blender, combine the ice cream, marshmallow cream, 1 crushed graham cracker, and milk.

3. Blend for 3 minutes in a milkshake mixer or 1 to 1½ minutes in a blender. The milkshake should be so thick that a straw stands up on its own in the middle of the shake.

4. Garnish with the remaining graham cracker.

death by chocolate milkshake

Now we're talkin' chocolate. Get the richest, fudgiest chocolate ice cream you can find. Combine it with chocolate syrup and, puh-leeze, not regular milk, but chocolate milk. This is as chocolate-y as you can get.

3 scoops chocolate ice cream

3 tablespoons chocolate syrup (Fox's U-Bet preferred)

¼ cup chocolate milk

1. In the cup of a milkshake mixer or the pitcher of a blender, combine the ice cream, chocolate syrup, and chocolate milk.

2. Blend for 3 minutes in a milkshake mixer or 1 to 1½ minutes in a blender. The milkshake should be so thick that a straw stands up on its own in the middle of the shake.

peaches *and* cream milkshake

It's as simple as it sounds. Just peach ice cream, vanilla ice cream, and milk.
If you want to throw in some fresh peaches, don't let us stop you!

2 scoops peach ice cream

1 scoop vanilla ice cream

¼ cup whole milk

1. In the cup of a milkshake mixer or the pitcher of a blender, combine the ice creams and milk.

2. Blend for 3 minutes in a milkshake mixer or 1 to 1½ minutes in a blender. The milkshake should be so thick that a straw stands up on its own in the middle of the shake.

"All that for me?"

chapter 10

divine
desserts

Saving the Best for Last

Eating a slice of apple pie isn't just about the delicious taste of cinnamon, apples, and crust—topped with vanilla ice cream—mixing in your mouth. At a diner, it's also about the way the hot coffee smells as it's poured, and the way your spoon clinks against the mug as you stir in a little cream and sugar. It's about the waitress saying "Heeeere you go!"—and the involuntary smile you get on your face when the slice is tossed down in front of you.

At home, that apple pie tastes just as good, especially if you're making the Mile-High Apple Pie from the Comfort Diner. This chapter is loaded with our enormous desserts and sweets, including pies, cookies, cakes, and muffins, our easiest treats for the time-strapped home cook.

I'm sure you know the saying: "Life is uncertain. Eat dessert first." Well, I'm not sure I would go that far. You might miss out on the bite of mac and cheese that melts away your troubles. So I'm more likely to say, "Life is great. Eat dessert with gusto."

perfect pie crust

First off, allow me to introduce the most indestructible pie dough you will ever meet. You can overmix it or give it to your kids to play with, and still it will make a delicious crust. You can even keep it in the freezer for up to three months. The high sugar content provides its strength, and the egg makes it tender. This recipe probably goes against everything you know about pie dough, but you know, I'm a rebel. And, yes, I do have a cause: tasty pastry.

2½ cups all-purpose flour

½ cup sugar

Pinch of salt

½ cup (1 stick) unsalted cold butter, cut into 1-inch cubes

1 large egg

1. In the bowl of a standing mixer, combine the flour, sugar, and salt. (A food processor is not recommended.) Add the butter and mix for 2 to 3 minutes, until the texture looks like crumbly sand. Add the egg and mix to combine thoroughly.

2. Turn the dough onto a sheet of floured waxed paper, and divide it in half. Set aside one half. Roll the working dough into a disc, about 1 inch wider than the pie pan.

3. Lift the waxed paper and turn it over so that the pie dough falls into the pan. Crimp the edges. Refrigerate for 30 minutes. If you are reserving the other half, form it into a thick disc and wrap it in plastic film. Freeze until needed. If you plan to use the second half for the top of a pie, roll it into a thick disc and refrigerate until needed.

4. For recipes that call for a prebaked pie shell, remove the pie pan from the refrigerator and press a sheet of aluminum foil down against the pie shell interior. Cover with pie weights or dried beans. Bake for 25 minutes in a preheated 350° oven. Remove the foil and weights, and bake for 5 to 7 minutes, until lightly browned.

pecan pie

Makes one 9-inch pie

When it comes to pecan pie, there is a very technical and scientific measure you must understand. It's called the "nut-to-goo" ratio. Like I said, it's very scientific. I like a ratio of about 3 to 1, and I think most people would agree. (And judging from the popularity of this pie, I think they do.) Be sure that when you're making this you have plenty of pecans. Don't skimp — if you do, the goo wins.

5 large eggs

1 cup sugar

½ cup (1 stick) unsalted butter, melted and cooled

1½ cups light corn syrup

3 cups whole pecans

1 unbaked Perfect Pie Crust (page 144), chilled for at least 1 hour

1. Preheat the oven to 350°F. In a mixing bowl, beat the eggs. Whisk the sugar into the eggs.

2. Whisk in the butter, then add the corn syrup and stir the filling thoroughly.

3. Fill the pie shell halfway with the pecans (reserve any extra for another use). Pour in the filling. Let the filling settle for 5 minutes, and add more if needed. The filling should reach the top edge of the crust.

4. Bake for 30 minutes. Then cover with foil and bake for an additional 45 minutes, until only the center jiggles slightly when shaken.

banana cream pie

I could slurp down a slice of this pie every night for dessert. That gooey center is just so smooth. This was a favorite dessert of mine as a kid, and it's still up there in my personal Top Ten. Plus, it's another diner must-have.

1 cup sugar

½ teaspoon salt

⅔ cup all-purpose flour

2 cups whole milk

1½ cups water

6 large egg yolks

1 prebaked Perfect Pie Crust (page 144)

2 cups sliced bananas (about 3 bananas)

2 cups or more whipped cream, to cover the pie

1. In a saucepan at medium-low heat, whisk together the sugar, salt, flour, milk, and water. Heat for about 5 minutes, until just warm to the touch and with no more flour lumps.

2. Add the egg yolks 1 at a time. Whisk constantly as you add them.

3. Bring the liquid to the boiling point, then reduce the heat and allow the cream mixture to simmer for 10 to 12 minutes, until thick and custardlike. Whisk frequently to be sure the mixture is not burning or thickening too early.

4. Arrange the bananas in the pie shell. Pour the cream mixture over the bananas.

5. Refrigerate until set. Finish with whipped cream on the top.

Cream pies aren't just for diners. They're for faces, too. C'mon, whats funnier than a pie in the face? Especially when it's a big-time, influential person who gets it! Activists have long used pie to make a political statement, but whatever point they're making, it's just pure slapstick humor. Here's a list of movers-and-shakers who've been "pied" over the years. Please note that the Comfort Diner does not condone such activity. (But we're still gonna laugh our pants off when we see it happen on television.)

Microsoft founder Bill Gates

Former Canadian Prime Minister Jean Chrétien

Economist Milton Friedman

United States UN chief negotiator Frank Loy

Former San Francisco mayor Willie Brown

Columnist William F. Buckley

Former New York mayor Abe Beame

Politician Ralph Nader

Film director Jean-Luc Godard

Former chief executive of Chevron Kenneth Derr

mile-high apple pie

A trip to a New England apple orchard in the fall is one of life's great joys. I love looking back on apple-picking excursions with my parents. This apple pie triggers those memories and really makes me smile. I hope it works for you, too. Just don't try to smile while you're chewing. I put so many apples in this dessert that there's practically a whole apple in every slice of pie. You can use less if you like, but I dare you — I double dog dare you — to use more.

2 unbaked Perfect Pie Crusts (page 144)

5 cups thin-sliced Granny Smith apples (3 to 4 unpeeled apples)

5 cups thin-sliced Gala apples (3 to 4 unpeeled apples)

¼ cup all-purpose flour

½ cup sugar, plus 3 tablespoons for sprinkling

1 tablespoon ground cinnamon

1. Preheat the oven to 350°F. Fit 1 pie shell in a pie pan (see the Perfect Pie Crust recipe for detailed instructions).

2. In a large bowl, toss together the apples, flour, sugar, and cinnamon. Pile the mixture into the pie shell.

3. Brush the crust edges with water. Roll out the second pie shell and place it over the apple mixture. Crimp the edges together. Cut slits in the top of the crust. Brush with water and sprinkle with the 3 tablespoons sugar.

4. Bake for 45 to 50 minutes, until golden brown.

blueberry muffins

If I tried to run a diner and didn't have a blueberry muffin, I'd be thrown in jail. Well, more or less. These are *filled* with berries and just plain delicious. Don't feel that you can use this batter only for blueberries. You can add in nuts, bananas, cranberries, or any crazy combo that you like.

1 cup (2 sticks) unsalted butter, softened

2 cups sugar, plus 2 tablespoons for sprinkling

4 large eggs

2 teaspoons vanilla extract

4 cups all-purpose flour

1 teaspoon salt

½ teaspoon baking soda

1½ cups sour cream

1 cup blueberries

1. Preheat the oven to 375° F. Grease 2 standard muffin tins.

2. In the bowl of a mixer, cream the butter, sugar, eggs, and vanilla. Add the flour, salt, and baking soda, and mix to combine.

3. Fold in the sour cream by hand, mixing only until incorporated. Fold in the berries.

4. Scoop 3-tablespoon dollops of batter into each muffin cup. Sprinkle ¼ teaspoon sugar on the top of each muffin.

5. Bake the muffins for 25 minutes, until they are cooked through and lightly golden. Allow the muffins to cool in the pan before serving.

russian coffee cake

Everyone knows the phrase "Easy as pie." Well, if they knew this recipe, they'd say "Easy as Russian Coffee Cake." Doesn't have quite the same ring, I know. But of all the recipes in this book, this is the one that will cause you the least trouble for the most wow-factor.

The one thing to remember in this recipe is that the pan must be very well greased. Do not be frugal at this step. Slather on the shortening or oil very liberally — the way you would sunscreen on your shoulders. At the diner, we use a vegetable oil spray that really works. Whatever you use, use plenty. Also, if you don't like raisins in your cake, just leave them out and double the amount of walnuts.

Filling

1 cup (unpacked) light brown sugar

¼ cup unsweetened cocoa powder

1 tablespoon ground cinnamon

¾ cup roughly chopped walnuts (optional)

¾ cup raisins (optional)

Cake

¾ cup (1½ sticks) unsalted butter, softened

1½ cups granulated sugar

3 large eggs

1 tablespoon vanilla extract

2 cups all-purpose flour

1½ tablespoons baking powder

1½ teaspoons baking soda

½ teaspoon salt

2 cups sour cream

1. Preheat the oven to 350°F. Prepare the filling in advance by mixing the brown sugar, cocoa, and cinnamon in a large bowl. Add the walnuts and raisins, if desired. Set aside. Grease a nonstick 12-cup capacity Bundt pan liberally with shortening, oil, or cooking spray.

2. In the bowl of a mixer, cream the butter, granulated sugar, eggs, and vanilla. Add the flour, baking powder, baking soda, and salt. Mix gently to combine. Fold in the sour cream.

3. Place 3 large scoops of the batter in the Bundt pan and spread it evenly.

4. Sprinkle ½ cup of the filling on the batter.

5. Repeat steps 3 and 4.

6. Finish with the remaining batter, spreading it evenly over the filling. Bake in the oven for 40 to 45 minutes, until a toothpick comes out clean. When done, invert to remove from the pan immediately and place on a cooling rack.

In the lingo of American food, anything that is made with sour cream is often described as "Russian." Otherwise, there's nothing particularly Russian about our coffee cake. And if you wanted to embellish it with other toppings or treats inside, you could give it the old college try. Sliced-up bananas inside instead of raisins would give you a tropical coffee cake. Sliced apples could make for a special autumn version. Or chocolate chips instead of cocoa for a "Swiss" version. And if you have your very own "house" filling, why not try adding that to the middle of the batter? For folks who prefer to stick to the recipe, here's a tip: the walnut, cocoa, and raisin filling keeps well. So if you like, you can make more than is needed, so that you can use it to top your muffins or other baked goods. And what in this world couldn't use a little extra dusting of sweetness?

rice pudding

Don't let the raisin issue divide your family or prevent you from making this cus-tard-y, ultracreamy dessert. You can make this with or without raisins. Or you could make a whole batch and put raisins in only half — like a pizza that's half plain and half pepperoni. Or you could make a game of it and put one raisin in. Who's gonna be the lucky raisin finder?

1 cup long-grain rice

½ teaspoon ground nutmeg

2 cups water

6 large eggs

2 cups sugar

3 tablespoons unsalted butter, melted and cooled

3 cups whole milk

3 cups heavy cream

1 teaspoon salt, plus a pinch

½ cup raisins (optional)

1 tablespoon ground cinnamon

1. Preheat the oven to 350°F. Butter a 9×12-inch baking dish. In a small pot, combine the rice, nutmeg, and water. Bring to a boil, then cover and simmer for 15 to 20 minutes, until the rice is tender. (Or cook according to package directions, adding the nutmeg.)

2. In a bowl, whisk the eggs. Add the sugar and melted butter; blend until evenly mixed and smooth.

3. In a separate large bowl, mix the milk and heavy cream. Add the 1 teaspoon salt. Whisk in the egg mixture.

4. Spread the rice around in the baking dish, then pour the liquid mixture over it. If using raisins, stir them in now. Sprinkle with the cinnamon and a pinch of salt. Place the baking dish inside a larger roasting pan. Fill the roasting pan with enough water so that the baking dish is sitting halfway in water.

5. Bake in the oven for 40 to 45 minutes, until the middle moves only slightly when shaken and the texture is custardlike.

grandma newell's peanut butter cookies

Makes about 3 dozen cookies

Our pastry chef, Lynn Septoff, got this recipe from her great grandmother, and it makes me really happy that we can use it. It's a tribute to grandmothers everywhere and it adds a homey element. I mean, really, that's the essence of comfort food: peanut butter cookies like a grandmother would make them.

1 cup (2 sticks) unsalted butter, softened

1 cup granulated sugar, plus 3 tablespoons for sprinkling

1 cup (unpacked) light brown sugar

1 cup peanut butter

2 large eggs

3 cups all-purpose flour

2 teaspoons baking soda

½ teaspoon salt

1. Preheat the oven to 350°F. Grease a cookie sheet or line with parchment paper.

2. In the bowl of a mixer, combine the butter, granulated sugar, brown sugar, and peanut butter. Add the eggs and combine. Add the flour, baking soda, and salt. Mix to combine.

3. Using your hands, roll 3 tablespoons of batter into balls. Flatten slightly into discs and place onto the prepared cookie sheet.

4. Score the cookies with fork marks and sprinkle each with ¼ teaspoon of sugar.

5. Bake in the oven for 7 to 8 minutes, depending on how you like them. For soft cookies, cook for 6 minutes, allowing the middles to be a little underdone. Transfer the cookies to racks and allow them to cool before serving.

chocolate chocolate chip cookies

Makes 2½ dozen cookies

Though diners are famous for showing off their cakes and muffins, cookies are just as important to us at the Comfort Diner. Nothing makes the world seem right like a delicious chocolate chip cookie dipped in milk. And if one kind of chocolate is good, isn't two even better? We mix good ol' chocolate chips into a rich chocolate batter. You could add a third if you want. (And send me a postcard to tell me how it is.)

1 cup (2 sticks) unsalted
    butter, softened

2 cups sugar

2½ teaspoons vanilla extract

2 large eggs

2½ cups all-purpose flour

¾ cup (heaping) unsweetened
    cocoa powder, sifted

1 teaspoon baking soda

¼ teaspoon salt

1¼ cups chocolate chips

1. Preheat the oven to 350°F. Grease a cookie sheet or line with parchment paper.

2. In a large bowl, cream the butter, sugar, and vanilla. Add the eggs and mix well.

3. In a smaller bowl, sift together the flour, cocoa, baking soda, and salt. Add the dry ingredients to the wet and mix to combine, then fold in the chips. Mix the dough by hand, if necessary.

4. Onto the prepared cookie sheet, place 2-tablespoon scoops of dough 2 inches apart.

5. Bake in the oven for 12 minutes. For softer cookies, cook for 10 minutes and allow the middles to be a little underdone. Transfer the cookies to racks and allow them to cool before serving.

Good Eats for Game Time

When entertaining centers around The Big Game — whether it's the World Series or the Super Bowl, the Little League Championship or the local high school rivalry — this menu will have the fans cheering for you.

Buffalo Wings (page 32) with Blue Cheese Dressing (page 129)

Three-Bean Vegetarian Chili (page 90)

Lively Tomato Salsa with chips (page 121)

Chocolate Chocolate Chip Cookies (page 154)

Diner Trivia

In diner speak, the British get some gentle ribbing. For tea with lemon, the jargon is "a spot with a twist." And for a toasted English muffin, get ready to hear the words: "Burn the British." If you happened to order that with jelly, you'll get it with some "shake."

index